Life Application Bible Studies
MARK

life

APPLICATION® BIBLE STUDIES

Part 1:
Complete text of Mark with study notes and features
from the *Life Application Study Bible*

Part 2:
Thirteen lessons for individual or group study

Study questions written and edited by

Dr. James C. Galvin
Rev. David R. Veerman
Dr. Bruce B. Barton
Daryl J. Lucas

mark

New Living
Translation®

Tyndale House Publishers, Inc.
Carol Stream, Illinois

Visit Tyndale online at www.newlivingtranslation.com and www.tyndale.com.

New Living Translation, NLT, the New Living Translation logo, *Life Application*, *Life App*, and the Life App logo are registered trademarks of Tyndale House Publishers, Inc.

Life Application Bible Studies: Mark

Copyright © 1999, 2009 by Tyndale House Publishers, Inc., Carol Stream, Illinois 60188. All rights reserved.

Life Application notes and features copyright © 1988, 1989, 1990, 1991, 1993, 1996, 2004 by Tyndale House Publishers, Inc., Carol Stream, Illinois 60188. Maps in text copyright © 1986, 1988 by Tyndale House Publishers, Inc. All rights reserved.

Cover photograph copyright © by Jupiterimages. All rights reserved.

The text of Mark is from the *Holy Bible,* New Living Translation, copyright © 1996, 2004, 2007 by Tyndale House Foundation. All rights reserved.

The text of the *Holy Bible,* New Living Translation, may be quoted in any form (written, visual, electronic, or audio) up to and inclusive of five hundred (500) verses without express written permission of the publisher, provided that the verses quoted do not account for more than twenty-five percent (25%) of the work in which they are quoted, and provided that acomplete book of the Bible is not quoted.

When the *Holy Bible,* New Living Translation, is quoted, one of the following credit lines must appear on the copyright page or title page of the work:

When quotations from the NLT text are used in nonsalable media, such as church bulletins, orders of service, newsletters, transparencies, or similar media, a complete copyright notice is not required, but the initials *NLT* must appear at the end of each quotation.

Quotations in excess of five hundred (500) verses or twenty-five percent (25%) of the work, or other permission requests, must be approved in writing by Tyndale House Publishers, Inc. Send requests by e-mail to: permission@tyndale.com or call 630-668-8300, ext. 5023.

Publication of any commentary or other Bible reference work produced for commercial sale that uses the New Living Translation requires written permission for use of the NLT text.

For information about special discounts for bulk purchases, please contact Tyndale House Publishers at csresponse@tyndale.com, or call 1-800-323-9400.

ISBN 978-1-4143-2650-4

Printed in the United States of America

23   22   21   20   19
9   8   7   6   5   4

CONTENTS

A NOTE TO READERS

The *Holy Bible,* New Living Translation, was first published in 1996. It quickly became one of the most popular Bible translations in the English-speaking world. While the NLT's influence was rapidly growing, the Bible Translation Committee determined that an additional investment in scholarly review and text refinement could make it even better. So shortly after its initial publication, the committee began an eight-year process with the purpose of increasing the level of the NLT's precision without sacrificing its easy-to-understand quality. This second-generation text was completed in 2004 and is reflected in this edition of the New Living Translation. An additional update with minor changes was subsequently introduced in 2007.

The goal of any Bible translation is to convey the meaning and content of the ancient Hebrew, Aramaic, and Greek texts as accurately as possible to contemporary readers. The challenge for our translators was to create a text that would communicate as clearly and powerfully to today's readers as the original texts did to readers and listeners in the ancient biblical world. The resulting translation is easy to read and understand, while also accurately communicating the meaning and content of the original biblical texts. The NLT is a general-purpose text especially good for study, devotional reading, and reading aloud in worship services.

We believe that the New Living Translation—which combines the latest biblical scholarship with a clear, dynamic writing style—will communicate God's word powerfully to all who read it. We publish it with the prayer that God will use it to speak his timeless truth to the church and the world in a fresh, new way.

The Publishers
October 2007

INTRODUCTION TO THE
NEW LIVING TRANSLATION

Translation Philosophy and Methodology

English Bible translations tend to be governed by one of two general translation theories. The first theory has been called "formal-equivalence," "literal," or "word-for-word" translation. According to this theory, the translator attempts to render each word of the original language into English and seeks to preserve the original syntax and sentence structure as much as possible in translation. The second theory has been called "dynamic-equivalence," "functional-equivalence," or "thought-for-thought" translation. The goal of this translation theory is to produce in English the closest natural equivalent of the message expressed by the original-language text, both in meaning and in style.

Both of these translation theories have their strengths. A formal-equivalence translation preserves aspects of the original text—including ancient idioms, term consistency, and original-language syntax—that are valuable for scholars and professional study. It allows a reader to trace formal elements of the original-language text through the English translation. A dynamic-equivalence translation, on the other hand, focuses on translating the message of the original-language text. It ensures that the meaning of the text is readily apparent to the contemporary reader. This allows the message to come through with immediacy, without requiring the reader to struggle with foreign idioms and awkward syntax. It also facilitates serious study of the text's message and clarity in both devotional and public reading.

The pure application of either of these translation philosophies would create translations at opposite ends of the translation spectrum. But in reality, all translations contain a mixture of these two philosophies. A purely formal-equivalence translation would be unintelligible in English, and a purely dynamic-equivalence translation would risk being unfaithful to the original. That is why translations shaped by dynamic-equivalence theory are usually quite literal when the original text is relatively clear, and the translations shaped by formal-equivalence theory are sometimes quite dynamic when the original text is obscure.

The translators of the New Living Translation set out to render the message of the original texts of Scripture into clear, contemporary English. As they did so, they kept the concerns of both formal-equivalence and dynamic-equivalence in mind. On the one hand, they translated as simply and literally as possible when that approach yielded an accurate, clear, and natural English text. Many words and phrases were rendered literally and consistently into English, preserving essential literary and rhetorical devices, ancient metaphors, and word choices that give structure to the text and provide echoes of meaning from one passage to the next.

On the other hand, the translators rendered the message more dynamically when the literal rendering was hard to understand, was misleading, or yielded archaic or foreign wording. They clarified difficult metaphors and terms to aid in the reader's understanding. The translators first struggled with the meaning of the words and phrases in the ancient context; then they rendered the message into clear, natural English. Their goal was to be both faithful to the ancient texts and eminently readable. The result is a translation that is both exegetically accurate and idiomatically powerful.

Translation Process and Team

To produce an accurate translation of the Bible into contemporary English, the translation team needed the skills necessary to enter into the thought patterns of the ancient authors and then to render their ideas, connotations, and effects into clear, contemporary English.

To begin this process, qualified biblical scholars were needed to interpret the meaning of the original text and to check it against our base English translation. In order to guard against personal and theological biases, the scholars needed to represent a diverse group of evangelicals who would employ the best exegetical tools. Then to work alongside the scholars, skilled English stylists were needed to shape the text into clear, contemporary English.

With these concerns in mind, the Bible Translation Committee recruited teams of scholars that represented a broad spectrum of denominations, theological perspectives, and backgrounds within the worldwide evangelical community. Each book of the Bible was assigned to three different scholars with proven expertise in the book or group of books to be reviewed. Each of these scholars made a thorough review of a base translation and submitted suggested revisions to the appropriate Senior Translator. The Senior Translator then reviewed and summarized these suggestions and proposed a first-draft revision of the base text. This draft served as the basis for several additional phases of exegetical and stylistic committee review. Then the Bible Translation Committee jointly reviewed and approved every verse of the final translation.

Throughout the translation and editing process, the Senior Translators and their scholar teams were given a chance to review the editing done by the team of stylists. This ensured that exegetical errors would not be introduced late in the process and that the entire Bible Translation Committee was happy with the final result. By choosing a team of qualified scholars and skilled stylists and by setting up a process that allowed their interaction throughout the process, the New Living Translation has been refined to preserve the essential formal elements of the original biblical texts, while also creating a clear, understandable English text.

The New Living Translation was first published in 1996. Shortly after its initial publication, the Bible Translation Committee began a process of further committee review and translation refinement. The purpose of this continued revision was to increase the level of precision without sacrificing the text's easy-to-understand quality. This second-edition text was completed in 2004, and an additional update with minor changes was subsequently introduced in 2007. This printing of the New Living Translation reflects the updated 2007 text.

Written to Be Read Aloud

It is evident in Scripture that the biblical documents were written to be read aloud, often in public worship (see Nehemiah 8; Luke 4:16-20; 1 Timothy 4:13; Revelation 1:3). It is still the case today that more people will hear the Bible read aloud in church than are likely to read it for themselves. Therefore, a new translation must communicate with clarity and power when it is read publicly. Clarity was a primary goal for the NLT translators, not only to facilitate private reading and understanding, but also to ensure that it would be excellent for public reading and make an immediate and powerful impact on any listener.

The Texts behind the New Living Translation

The Old Testament translators used the Masoretic Text of the Hebrew Bible as represented in *Biblia Hebraica Stuttgartensia* (1977), with its extensive system of textual notes; this is an update of Rudolf Kittel's *Biblia Hebraica* (Stuttgart, 1937). The translators also further compared the Dead Sea Scrolls, the Septuagint and other Greek manuscripts, the Samaritan Pentateuch, the Syriac Peshitta, the Latin Vulgate, and any other versions or manuscripts that shed light on the meaning of difficult passages.

The New Testament translators used the two standard editions of the Greek New Testament: the *Greek New Testament,* published by the United Bible Societies (UBS, fourth revised edition, 1993), and *Novum Testamentum Graece,* edited by Nestle and Aland (NA, twenty-seventh edition, 1993). These two editions, which have the same text but differ in punctuation and textual notes, represent, for the most part, the best in modern textual scholarship. However, in cases where strong textual or other scholarly evidence supported the decision, the translators sometimes chose to differ from the UBS and NA Greek texts and followed variant readings found in other ancient witnesses. Significant textual variants of this sort are always noted in the textual notes of the New Living Translation.

Translation Issues

The translators have made a conscious effort to provide a text that can be easily understood by the typical reader of modern English. To this end, we sought to use only vocabulary and language structures in common use today. We avoided using language likely to become quickly dated or that reflects only a narrow subdialect of English, with the goal of making the New Living Translation as broadly useful and timeless as possible.

But our concern for readability goes beyond the concerns of vocabulary and sentence structure. We are also concerned about historical and cultural barriers to understanding the Bible, and we have sought to translate terms shrouded in history and culture in ways that can be immediately understood. To this end:

- We have converted ancient weights and measures (for example, "ephah" [a unit of dry volume] or "cubit" [a unit of length]) to modern English (American) equivalents, since the ancient measures are not generally meaningful to today's readers. Then in the textual footnotes we offer the literal Hebrew, Aramaic, or Greek measures, along with modern metric equivalents.
- Instead of translating ancient currency values literally, we have expressed them in common terms that communicate the message. For example, in the Old Testament, "ten shekels of silver" becomes "ten pieces of silver" to convey the intended message. In the New Testament, we have often translated the "denarius" as "the normal daily wage" to facilitate understanding. Then a footnote offers: "Greek *a denarius,* the payment for a full day's labor." In general, we give a clear English rendering and then state the literal Hebrew, Aramaic, or Greek in a textual footnote.
- Since the names of Hebrew months are unknown to most contemporary readers, and since the Hebrew lunar calendar fluctuates from year to year in relation to the solar calendar used today, we have looked for clear ways to communicate the time of year the Hebrew months (such as Abib) refer to. When an expanded or interpretive rendering is given in the text, a textual note gives the literal rendering. Where it is possible to define a specific ancient date in terms of our modern calendar, we use modern dates in the text. A textual footnote then gives the literal Hebrew date and states the rationale for our rendering. For example, Ezra 6:15 pinpoints the date when the postexilic Temple was completed in Jerusalem: "the third day of the month Adar." This was during the sixth year of King Darius's reign (that is, 515 B.C.). We have translated that date as March 12, with a footnote giving the Hebrew and identifying the year as 515 B.C.
- Since ancient references to the time of day differ from our modern methods of denoting time, we have used renderings that are instantly understandable to the modern reader. Accordingly, we have rendered specific times of day by using approximate equivalents in terms of our common "o'clock" system. On occasion, translations such as "at dawn the next morning" or "as the sun was setting" have been used when the biblical reference is more general.
- When the meaning of a proper name (or a wordplay inherent in a proper name) is relevant to the message of the text, its meaning is often illuminated with a textual footnote. For example, in Exodus 2:10 the text reads: "The princess named him Moses, for she explained, 'I lifted him out of the water.' " The accompanying footnote reads: "*Moses* sounds like a Hebrew term that means 'to lift out.' "
  Sometimes, when the actual meaning of a name is clear, that meaning is included in parentheses within the text itself. For example, the text at Genesis 16:11 reads: "You are to name him Ishmael *(which means 'God hears'),* for the LORD has heard your cry of distress." Since the original hearers and readers would have instantly understood the meaning of the name "Ishmael," we have provided modern readers with the same information so they can experience the text in a similar way.
- Many words and phrases carry a great deal of cultural meaning that was obvious to the original readers but needs explanation in our own culture. For example, the phrase "they beat their breasts" (Luke 23:48) in ancient times meant that people were very upset, often in mourning. In our translation we chose to translate this phrase dynamically for clarity: "They went home *in deep sorrow.*" Then we included a footnote with the literal Greek, which reads: "Greek *went home beating their breasts.*" In other similar cases, however, we have sometimes chosen to illuminate the existing literal expression to make it immediately understandable. For example, here we might have expanded the literal Greek phrase to read: "They went home

beating their breasts *in sorrow."* If we had done this, we would not have included a textual footnote, since the literal Greek clearly appears in translation.

- Metaphorical language is sometimes difficult for contemporary readers to understand, so at times we have chosen to translate or illuminate the meaning of a metaphor. For example, the ancient poet writes, "Your neck is *like* the tower of David" (Song of Songs 4:4). We have rendered it "Your neck is *as beautiful as* the tower of David" to clarify the intended positive meaning of the simile. Another example comes in Ecclesiastes 12:3, which can be literally rendered: "Remember him . . . when the grinding women cease because they are few, and the women who look through the windows see dimly." We have rendered it: "Remember him before your teeth—your few remaining servants—stop grinding; and before your eyes—the women looking through the windows—see dimly." We clarified such metaphors only when we believed a typical reader might be confused by the literal text.

- When the content of the original language text is poetic in character, we have rendered it in English poetic form. We sought to break lines in ways that clarify and highlight the relationships between phrases of the text. Hebrew poetry often uses parallelism, a literary form where a second phrase (or in some instances a third or fourth) echoes the initial phrase in some way. In Hebrew parallelism, the subsequent parallel phrases continue, while also furthering and sharpening, the thought expressed in the initial line or phrase. Whenever possible, we sought to represent these parallel phrases in natural poetic English.

- The Greek term *hoi Ioudaioi* is literally translated "the Jews" in many English translations. In the Gospel of John, however, this term doesn't always refer to the Jewish people generally. In some contexts, it refers more particularly to the Jewish religious leaders. We have attempted to capture the meaning in these different contexts by using terms such as "the people" (with a footnote: Greek *the Jewish people*) or "the Jewish leaders," where appropriate.

- One challenge we faced was how to translate accurately the ancient biblical text that was originally written in a context where male-oriented terms were used to refer to humanity generally. We needed to respect the nature of the ancient context while also trying to make the translation clear to a modern audience that tends to read male-oriented language as applying only to males. Often the original text, though using masculine nouns and pronouns, clearly intends that the message be applied to both men and women. A typical example is found in the New Testament letters, where the believers are called "brothers" (*adelphoi*). Yet it is clear from the content of these letters that they were addressed to all the believers—male and female. Thus, we have usually translated this Greek word as "brothers and sisters" in order to represent the historical situation more accurately.

   We have also been sensitive to passages where the text applies generally to human beings or to the human condition. In some instances we have used plural pronouns (they, them) in place of the masculine singular (he, him). For example, a traditional rendering of Proverbs 22:6 is: "Train up a child in the way he should go, and when he is old he will not turn from it." We have rendered it: "Direct your children onto the right path, and when they are older, they will not leave it." At times, we have also replaced third person pronouns with the second person to ensure clarity. A traditional rendering of Proverbs 26:27 is: "He who digs a pit will fall into it, and he who rolls a stone, it will come back on him." We have rendered it: "If you set a trap for others, you will get caught in it yourself. If you roll a boulder down on others, it will crush you instead."

   We should emphasize, however, that all masculine nouns and pronouns used to represent God (for example, "Father") have been maintained without exception. All decisions of this kind have been driven by the concern to reflect accurately the intended meaning of the original texts of Scripture.

Lexical Consistency in Terminology

For the sake of clarity, we have translated certain original-language terms consistently, especially within synoptic passages and for commonly repeated rhetorical phrases, and within certain word categories such as divine names and non-theological technical terminology (e.g., liturgical, legal, cultural, zoological, and botanical terms). For theological terms, we have allowed a greater semantic range of acceptable English words or phrases for a single Hebrew or Greek word. We have avoided some theological terms that are not readily understood by many modern readers. For example, we avoided using words such as "justification" and "sanctification," which are carryovers from Latin translations. In place of these words, we have provided renderings such as "made right with God" and "made holy."

The Spelling of Proper Names

Many individuals in the Bible, especially the Old Testament, are known by more than one name (e.g., Uzziah/Azariah). For the sake of clarity, we have tried to use a single spelling for any one individual, footnoting the literal spelling whenever we differ from it. This is especially helpful in delineating the kings of Israel and Judah. King Joash/Jehoash of Israel has been consistently called Jehoash, while King Joash/Jehoash of Judah is called Joash. A similar distinction has been used to distinguish between Joram/Jehoram of Israel and Joram/Jehoram of Judah. All such decisions were made with the goal of clarifying the text for the reader. When the ancient biblical writers clearly had a theological purpose in their choice of a variant name (e.g., Esh-baal/Ishbosheth), the different names have been maintained with an explanatory footnote.

For the names Jacob and Israel, which are used interchangeably for both the individual patriarch and the nation, we generally render it "Israel" when it refers to the nation and "Jacob" when it refers to the individual. When our rendering of the name differs from the underlying Hebrew text, we provide a textual footnote, which includes this explanation: "The names 'Jacob' and 'Israel' are often interchanged throughout the Old Testament, referring sometimes to the individual patriarch and sometimes to the nation."

The Rendering of Divine Names

All appearances of *'el, 'elohim,* or *'eloah* have been translated "God," except where the context demands the translation "god(s)." We have generally rendered the tetragrammaton (*YHWH*) consistently as "the Lord," utilizing a form with small capitals that is common among English translations. This will distinguish it from the name *'adonai,* which we render "Lord." When *'adonai* and *YHWH* appear together, we have rendered it "Sovereign Lord." This also distinguishes *'adonai YHWH* from cases where *YHWH* appears with *'elohim,* which is rendered "Lord God." When *YH* (the short form of *YHWH*) and *YHWH* appear together, we have rendered it "Lord God." When *YHWH* appears with the term *tseba'oth,* we have rendered it "Lord of Heaven's Armies" to translate the meaning of the name. In a few cases, we have utilized the transliteration, *Yahweh,* when the personal character of the name is being invoked in contrast to another divine name or the name of some other god (for example, see Exodus 3:15; 6:2-3).

In the Gospels and Acts, the Greek word *christos* has been translated as "Messiah" when the context assumes a Jewish audience. When a Gentile audience can be assumed (which is consistently the case in the Epistles and Revelation), *christos* has been translated as "Christ." The Greek word *kurios* is consistently translated "Lord," except that it is translated "Lord" wherever the New Testament text explicitly quotes from the Old Testament, and the text there has it in small capitals.

Textual Footnotes

The New Living Translation provides several kinds of textual footnotes, all designated in the text with an asterisk:

- When for the sake of clarity the NLT renders a difficult or potentially confusing phrase dynamically, we generally give the literal rendering in a textual footnote. This allows the reader to see the literal source of our dynamic rendering and how our translation relates to other more literal translations. These notes are prefaced with "Hebrew," "Aramaic," or "Greek," identifying the language of the underlying source text. For example, in Acts 2:42 we translated the literal "breaking of bread" (from the Greek) as "the Lord's Supper" to clarify that this verse refers to the ceremonial practice of the church rather than just an ordinary meal. Then we attached a footnote to "the Lord's Supper," which reads: "Greek *the breaking of bread.*"

- Textual footnotes are also used to show alternative renderings, prefaced with the word "Or." These normally occur for passages where an aspect of the meaning is debated. On occasion, we also provide notes on words or phrases that represent a departure from long-standing tradition. These notes are prefaced with "Traditionally rendered." For example, the footnote to the translation "serious skin disease" at Leviticus 13:2 says: "Traditionally rendered *leprosy*. The Hebrew word used throughout this passage is used to describe various skin diseases."

- When our translators follow a textual variant that differs significantly from our standard Hebrew or Greek texts (listed earlier), we document that difference with a footnote. We also footnote cases when the NLT excludes a passage that is included in the Greek text known as the *Textus Receptus* (and familiar to readers through its translation in the King James Version). In such cases, we offer a translation of the excluded text in a footnote, even though it is generally recognized as a later addition to the Greek text and not part of the original Greek New Testament.

- All Old Testament passages that are quoted in the New Testament are identified by a textual footnote at the New Testament location. When the New Testament clearly quotes from the reek translation of the Old Testament, and when it differs significantly in wording from the Hebrew text, we also place a textual footnote at the Old Testament location. This note includes a rendering of the Greek version, along with a cross-reference to the New Testament passage(s) where it is cited (for example, see notes on Psalms 8:2; 53:3; Proverbs 3:12).

- Some textual footnotes provide cultural and historical information on places, things, and people in the Bible that are probably obscure to modern readers. Such notes should aid the reader in understanding the message of the text. For example, in Acts 12:1, "King Herod" is named in this translation as "King Herod Agrippa" and is identified in a footnote as being "the nephew of Herod Antipas and a grandson of Herod the Great."

- When the meaning of a proper name (or a wordplay inherent in a proper name) is relevant to the meaning of the text, it is either illuminated with a textual footnote or included within parentheses in the text itself. For example, the footnote concerning the name "Eve" at Genesis 3:20 reads: "*Eve* sounds like a Hebrew term that means 'to give life.' " This wordplay in the Hebrew illuminates the meaning of the text, which goes on to say that Eve "would be the mother of all who live."

AS WE SUBMIT this translation for publication, we recognize that any translation of the Scriptures is subject to limitations and imperfections. Anyone who has attempted to communicate the richness of God's Word into another language will realize it is impossible to make a perfect translation. Recognizing these limitations, we sought God's guidance and wisdom throughout this project. Now we pray that he will accept our efforts and use this translation for the benefit of the church and of all people.

We pray that the New Living Translation will overcome some of the barriers of history, culture, and language that have kept people from reading and understanding God's Word. We hope that readers unfamiliar with the Bible will find the words clear and easy to understand and that readers well versed in the Scriptures will gain a fresh perspective. We pray that readers will gain insight and wisdom for living, but most of all that they will meet the God of the Bible and be forever changed by knowing him.

The Bible Translation Committee
October 2007

WHY THE
LIFE APPLICATION STUDY BIBLE
IS UNIQUE

Have you ever opened your Bible and asked the following:

- What does this passage really mean?
- How does it apply to my life?
- Why does some of the Bible seem irrelevant?
- What do these ancient cultures have to do with today?
- I love God; why can't I understand what he is saying to me through his word?
- What's going on in the lives of these Bible people?

Many Christians do not read the Bible regularly. Why? Because in the pressures of daily living they cannot find a connection between the timeless principles of Scripture and the ever-present problems of day-by-day living.

God urges us to apply his word (Isaiah 42:23; 1 Corinthians 10:11; 2 Thessalonians 3:4), but too often we stop at accumulating Bible knowledge. This is why the *Life Application Study Bible* was developed—to show how to put into practice what we have learned.

Applying God's word is a vital part of one's relationship with God; it is the evidence that we are obeying him. The difficulty in applying the Bible is not with the Bible itself, but with the reader's inability to bridge the gap between the past and present, the conceptual and practical. When we don't or can't do this, spiritual dryness, shallowness, and indifference are the results.

The words of Scripture itself cry out to us, "But don't just listen to God's word. You must do what it says. Otherwise, you are only fooling yourselves" (James 1:22). The *Life Application Study Bible* helps us to obey God's word. Developed by an interdenominational team of pastors, scholars, family counselors, and a national organization dedicated to promoting God's word and spreading the gospel, the *Life Application Study Bible* took many years to complete. All the work was reviewed by several renowned theologians under the directorship of Dr. Kenneth Kantzer.

The *Life Application Study Bible* does what a good resource Bible should: It helps you understand the context of a passage, gives important background and historical information, explains difficult words and phrases, and helps you see the interrelationship of Scripture. But it does much more. The *Life Application Study Bible* goes deeper into God's word, helping you discover the timeless truth being communicated, see the relevance for your life, and make a personal application. While some study Bibles attempt application, over 75 percent of this Bible is application oriented. The notes answer the questions "So what?" and "What does this passage mean to me, my family, my friends, my job, my neighborhood, my church, my country?"

Imagine reading a familiar passage of Scripture and gaining fresh insight, as if it were the first time you had ever read it. How much richer your life would be if you left each Bible reading with a new perspective and a small change for the better. A small change every day adds up to a changed life—and that is the very purpose of Scripture.

WHAT IS APPLICATION?

The best way to define application is to first determine what it is *not*. Application is *not* just accumulating knowledge. Accumulating knowledge helps us discover and understand facts and concepts, but it stops there. History is filled with philosophers who knew what the Bible said but failed to apply it to their lives, keeping them from believing and changing. Many think that understanding is the end goal of Bible study, but it is really only the beginning.

Application is *not* just illustration. Illustration only tells us how someone else handled a similar situation. While we may empathize with that person, we still have little direction for our personal situation.

Application is *not* just making a passage "relevant." Making the Bible relevant only helps us to see that the same lessons that were true in Bible times are true today; it does not show us how to apply them to the problems and pressures of our individual lives.

What, then, is application? Application begins by knowing and understanding God's word and its timeless truths. *But you cannot stop there.* If you do, God's word may not change your life, and it may become dull, difficult, tedious, and tiring. A good application focuses the truth of God's word, shows the reader what to do about what is being read, and motivates the reader to respond to what God is teaching. All three are essential to application.

Application is putting into practice what we already know (see Mark 4:24 and Hebrews 5:14) and answering the question "So what?" by confronting us with the right questions and motivating us to take action (see 1 John 2:5-6 and James 2:26). Application is deeply personal—unique for each individual. It makes a relevant truth a personal truth and involves developing a strategy and action plan to live your life in harmony with the Bible. It is the biblical "how to" of life.

You may ask, "How can your application notes be relevant to my life?" Each application note has three parts: (1) an *explanation*, which ties the note directly to the Scripture passage and sets up the truth that is being taught; (2) the *bridge*, which explains the timeless truth and makes it relevant for today; (3) the *application*, which shows you how to take the timeless truth and apply it to your personal situation. No note, by itself, can apply Scripture directly to your life. It can only teach, direct, lead, guide, inspire, recommend, and urge. It can give you the resources and direction you need to apply the Bible, but only you can take these resources and put them into practice.

A good note, therefore should not only give you knowledge and understanding but point you to application. Before you buy any kind of resource study Bible, you should evaluate the notes and ask the following questions: (1) Does the note contain enough information to help me understand the point of the Scripture passage? (2) Does the note assume I know more than I do? (3) Does the note avoid denominational bias? (4) Do the notes touch most of life's experiences? (5) Does the note help me apply God's word?

FEATURES OF THE
LIFE APPLICATION STUDY BIBLE

NOTES

In addition to providing the reader with many application notes, the *Life Application Study Bible* also offers several kinds of explanatory notes, which help the reader understand culture, history, context, difficult-to-understand passages, background, places, theological concepts, and the relationship of various passages in Scripture to other passages.

BOOK INTRODUCTIONS

Each book introduction is divided into several easy-to-find parts:

Timeline. A guide that puts the Bible book into its historical setting. It lists the key events and the dates when they occurred.

Vital Statistics. A list of straight facts about the book—those pieces of information you need to know at a glance.

Overview. A summary of the book with general lessons and applications that can be learned from the book as a whole.

Blueprint. The outline of the book. It is printed in easy-to-understand language and is designed for easy memorization. To the right of each main heading is a key lesson that is taught in that particular section.

Megathemes. A section that gives the main themes of the Bible book, explains their significance, and then tells you why they are still important for us today.

Map. If included, this shows the key places found in that book and retells the story of the book from a geographical point of view.

OUTLINE

The *Life Application Study Bible* has a new, custom-made outline that was designed specifically from an application point of view. Several unique features should be noted:

1. To avoid confusion and to aid memory work, the book outline has only three levels for headings. Main outline heads are marked with a capital letter. Subheads are marked by a number. Minor explanatory heads have no letter or number.

2. Each main outline head marked by a letter also has a brief paragraph below it summarizing the Bible text and offering a general application.

3. Parallel passages are listed where they apply.

PERSONALITY PROFILES

Among the unique features of this Bible are the profiles of key Bible people, including their strengths and weaknesses, greatest accomplishments and mistakes, and key lessons from their lives.

MAPS
The *Life Application Study Bible* has a thorough and comprehensive Bible atlas built right into the book. There are two kinds of maps: a book-introduction map, telling the story of the book, and thumbnail maps in the notes, plotting most geographic movements.

CHARTS AND DIAGRAMS
Many charts and diagrams are included to help the reader better visualize difficult concepts or relationships. Most charts not only present the needed information but show the significance of the information as well.

CROSS-REFERENCES
An updated, exhaustive cross-reference system in the margins of the Bible text helps the reader find related passages quickly.

TEXTUAL NOTES
Directly related to the text of the New Living Translation, the textual notes provide explanations on certain wording in the translation, alternate translations, and information about readings in the ancient manuscripts.

HIGHLIGHTED NOTES
In each Bible study lesson, you will be asked to read specific notes as part of your preparation. These notes have each been highlighted by a bullet (•) so that you can find them easily.

MARK

MARK

VITAL STATISTICS

PURPOSE:
To present the person, work, and teachings of Jesus

AUTHOR:
John Mark. He was not one of the 12 disciples, but he accompanied Paul on his first missionary journey (Acts 13:13).

ORIGINAL AUDIENCE:
The Christians in Rome, where the Gospel was written

DATE WRITTEN:
Between A.D. 55 and 65

SETTING:
The Roman Empire under Tiberius Caesar. The empire, with its common language and excellent transportation and communication systems, was ripe to hear Jesus' message, which spread quickly from nation to nation.

KEY VERSE:
"For even the Son of Man came not to be served but to serve others and to give his life as a ransom for many" (10:45).

KEY PEOPLE:
Jesus, the 12 disciples, Pilate, the Jewish religious leaders

KEY PLACES:
Capernaum, Nazareth, Caesarea Philippi, Jericho, Bethany, Mount of Olives, Jerusalem, Golgotha

SPECIAL FEATURES:
Mark was probably the first Gospel written. The other Gospels quote all but 31 verses of Mark. Mark records more miracles than does any other Gospel.

WE'RE number one! . . . The greatest, strongest, prettiest . . . champions! Daily such proclamations boldly assert claims of supremacy. Everyone wants to be associated with a winner. Losers are those who finish less than first. In direct contrast are the words of Jesus: "And whoever wants to be first must be the slave of everyone else. For even the Son of Man came here not to be served but to serve others and to give his life as a ransom for many" (10:44, 45). Jesus *is* the greatest—God incarnate, our Messiah—but he entered history as a servant.

This is the message of Mark. Written to encourage Roman Christians and to prove beyond a doubt that Jesus is the Messiah, Mark presents a rapid succession of vivid pictures of Jesus in action—his true identity revealed by what he does, not necessarily by what he says. It is Jesus on the move.

Omitting the birth of Jesus, Mark begins with John the Baptist's preaching. Then, moving quickly past Jesus' baptism, temptation in the wilderness, and call of the disciples, Mark takes us directly into Jesus' public ministry. We see Jesus confronting a demon, healing a man with leprosy, and forgiving and healing the paralyzed man lowered into Jesus' presence by friends.

Next, Jesus calls Matthew (Levi) and has dinner with him and his questionable associates. This initiates the conflict with the Pharisees and other religious leaders, who condemn Jesus for eating with sinners and breaking the Sabbath.

In chapter 4, Mark pauses to give a sample of Jesus' teaching—the parable of the farmer and the illustration of the mustard seed—and then plunges back into the action. Jesus calms the waves, drives out demons, and raises Jairus's daughter from the dead.

After returning to Nazareth for a few days and experiencing rejection in his hometown, Jesus commissions the disciples to spread the Good News everywhere. Opposition from Herod and the Pharisees increases, and John the Baptist is beheaded. But Jesus continues to move, feeding 5,000, reaching out to the woman from Syrian Phoenicia, healing the deaf man, and feeding 4,000.

Finally, it is time to reveal his true identity to the disciples. Do they really know who Jesus is? Peter proclaims him Messiah but then promptly shows that he does not understand Jesus' mission. After the Transfiguration, Jesus continues to teach and heal, confronting the Pharisees about divorce and the rich young man about eternal life. Blind Bartimaeus is healed.

Events move rapidly toward a climax. The Last Supper, the betrayal, the Crucifixion, and the Resurrection are dramatically portrayed, along with more examples of Jesus' teachings. Mark shows us Jesus—moving, serving, sacrificing, and saving! As you read Mark, be ready for action, be open for God's move in your life, and be challenged to move into your world to serve.

Tiberius Caesar becomes emperor 14		*John's ministry begins 26*	*Jesus begins his ministry 26/27*	*Jesus chooses twelve disciples 28*	*Jesus feeds 5,000 29*	*Jesus is crucified, rises again, and ascends 30*

THE BLUEPRINT

A. BIRTH AND PREPARATION OF JESUS, THE SERVANT (1:1–13)

Jesus did not arrive unannounced or unexpected. The Old Testament prophets had clearly predicted the coming of a great one, sent by God himself, who would offer salvation and eternal peace to Israel and the entire world. Then came John the Baptist, who announced that the long-awaited Messiah had finally come and would soon be among the people. In God's work in the world today, Jesus does not come unannounced or unexpected. Yet many still reject him. We have the witness of the Bible, but some choose to ignore it, just as many ignored John the Baptist in his day.

B. MESSAGE AND MINISTRY OF JESUS, THE SERVANT (1:14—13:37)
   1. Jesus' ministry in Galilee
   2. Jesus' ministry beyond Galilee
   3. Jesus' ministry in Jerusalem

Jesus had all the power of God: He raised the dead, gave sight to the blind, restored deformed bodies, and quieted stormy seas. But with all this power, Jesus came to humanity as a servant. We can use his life as a pattern for how to live today. As Jesus served God and others, so should we.

C. DEATH AND RESURRECTION OF JESUS, THE SERVANT (14:1—16:20)

Jesus came as a servant, so many did not recognize or acknowledge him as the Messiah. We must be careful that we also don't reject God or his will because he doesn't quite fit our image of what God should be.

MEGATHEMES

THEME	EXPLANATION	IMPORTANCE
Jesus Christ	Jesus Christ alone is the Son of God. In Mark, Jesus demonstrates his divinity by overcoming disease, demons, and death. Although he had the power to be king of the earth, Jesus chose to obey the Father and die for us.	When Jesus rose from the dead, he proved that he was God, that he could forgive sin, and that he has the power to change our lives. By trusting in him for forgiveness, we can begin a new life with him as our guide.
Servant	As the Messiah, Jesus fulfilled the prophecies of the Old Testament by coming to earth. He did not come as a conquering king; he came as a servant. He helped people by telling them about God and healing them. Even more, by giving his life as a sacrifice for sin, he performed the ultimate act of service.	Because of Jesus' example, we should be willing to serve God and others. Real greatness in Christ's Kingdom is shown by service and sacrifice. Ambition or love of power or position should not be our motive; instead, we should do God's work because we love him.
Miracles	Mark records more of Jesus' miracles than sermons. Jesus is clearly a man of power and action, not just words. Jesus did miracles to convince the people who he was and to confirm to the disciples his true identity— God.	The more convinced we become that Jesus is God, the more we will see his power and his love. His mighty works show us he is able to save anyone regardless of his or her past. His miracles of forgiveness bring healing, wholeness, and changed lives to those who trust him.
Spreading the Gospel	Jesus directed his public ministry to the Jews first. When the Jewish leaders opposed him, Jesus also went to the non-Jewish world, healing and preaching. Roman soldiers, Syrians, and other Gentiles heard the Good News. Many believed and followed him. Jesus' final message to his disciples challenged them to go into all the world and preach the gospel of salvation.	Jesus crossed national, racial, and economic barriers to spread his Good News. Jesus' message of faith and forgiveness is for the whole world—not just our church, neighborhood, or nation. We must reach out beyond our own people and needs to fulfill the worldwide vision of Jesus Christ so that people everywhere may hear this great message and be saved from sin and death.

A. BIRTH AND PREPARATION OF JESUS, THE SERVANT (1:1–13)

Mark, the shortest of the four Gospels, opens with Jesus' baptism and temptation. Moving right into action, Mark quickly prepares us for Christ's ministry. The Gospel of Mark is concise, straightforward, and chronological.

John the Baptist Prepares the Way for Jesus (**16**/Matthew 3:1-12; Luke 3:1-18)

1 This is the Good News about Jesus the Messiah, the Son of God.* It began ²just as the prophet Isaiah had written:

"Look, I am sending my messenger ahead of you,
     and he will prepare your way.*
³ He is a voice shouting in the wilderness,
'Prepare the way for the LORD's coming!
     Clear the road for him!'*"

⁴This messenger was John the Baptist. He was in the wilderness and preached that people should be baptized to show that they had repented of their sins and turned to God to be forgiven. ⁵All of Judea, including all the people of Jerusalem, went out to see and hear John. And when they confessed their sins, he baptized them in the Jordan River. ⁶His clothes were woven from coarse camel hair, and he wore a leather belt around his waist. For food he ate locusts and wild honey.

⁷John announced: "Someone is coming soon who is greater than I am—so much greater that I'm not even worthy to stoop down like a slave and untie the straps of his sandals. ⁸I baptize you with* water, but he will baptize you with the Holy Spirit!"

1:1 Some manuscripts do not include *the Son of God.* **1:2** Mal 3:1. **1:3** Isa 40:3 (Greek version). **1:8** Or *in;* also in 1:8b.

1:1	Ps 2:7 / Matt 1:1 / John 1:34 / 1 Jn 4:15
1:2-3	†Isa 40:3 / †Mal 3:1 / John 1:23
1:4	Acts 13:24; 19:4
1:6	Lev 11:22 / 2 Kgs 1:8 / Zech 13:4
1:7	Acts 13:25
1:8	Joel 2:28 / Acts 2:4; 10:45; 11:16

1:1 When you experience the excitement of a big event, you naturally want to tell someone. Telling the story can bring back that original thrill as you relive the experience. Reading Mark's first words, you can sense his excitement. Picture yourself in the crowd as Jesus heals and teaches. Imagine yourself as one of the disciples. Respond to his words of love and encouragement. And remember that Jesus came for us who live today as well as for those who lived 2,000 years ago.

• **1:1** Mark was not one of the 12 disciples of Jesus, but he probably knew Jesus personally. Mark wrote his Gospel in the form of a fast-paced story, like a popular novel. The book portrays Jesus as a man who backed up his words with action that constantly proved who he is—the Son of God. Because Mark wrote his Gospel for Christians in Rome, where many gods were worshiped, he wanted his readers to know that Jesus is *the one true* Son of God.

Without God's revelation, our finite minds cannot comprehend the infinite. But because of what we know about Jesus (thanks to writers like Mark), we can understand what God is like. Mark gave the "punch line" of his Gospel in the very first verse, but both Jesus' enemies and his disciples would not get it until Jesus' resurrection. For us who read Mark today, the message is clear that we must not ignore or reject Jesus Christ.

1:2, 3 Isaiah was one of the greatest prophets of the Old Testament. The second half of the book of Isaiah is devoted to the promise of salvation. Isaiah wrote about the coming of the Messiah, Jesus Christ, and the man who would announce his coming, John the Baptist. John's call to "clear the road for him" meant that people should give up their selfish way of living, renounce their sins, seek God's forgiveness, and establish a relationship with God by believing and obeying his words as found in Scripture (Isaiah 1:18-20; 57:15).

1:2, 3 Mark 1:2, 3 is a composite quotation, taken first from Malachi 3:1 and then from Isaiah 40:3.

• **1:2-4** Hundreds of years earlier, the prophet Isaiah had predicted that John the Baptist and Jesus would come. Isaiah's words comforted many people as they looked forward to the Messiah, and knowing that God keeps his promises can comfort you, too. As you read the book of Mark, realize that it is more than just a story; it is part of God's Word. In it God is revealing to you his plans for human history—and offering the Good News of his salvation to you.

1:3 John the Baptist prepared the way for Jesus. People who do not know Jesus need to be prepared to meet him. We can "prepare the way" by explaining their need for forgiveness, demonstrating Christ's teaching by our conduct, and telling them how Christ can give their lives meaning. We can "clear the road for him" by correcting misconceptions that might be hindering people form approaching Christ. Someone you know may be open to a relationship with Christ. What can you do to prepare the way for this person?

1:4 Why does the Gospel of Mark begin with the story of John the Baptist and not mention the story of Jesus' birth? Important Roman officials of this day were always preceded by an announcer or herald. When the herald arrived in town, the people knew that someone of prominence would soon arrive. Because Mark's audience was primarily Roman Christians, he began his book with John the Baptist, whose mission it was to announce the coming of Jesus, the most important man who ever lived. Roman Christians would have been less interested in Jesus' birth than in this messenger who prepared the way.

1:4 In John's ministry, baptism was a visible sign that a person had decided to change his or her life, giving up a sinful and selfish way of living and turning to God. John took a known custom and gave it new meaning. The Jews often baptized non-Jews who had converted to Judaism. But to baptize a Jew as a sign of repentance was a radical departure from Jewish custom. The early Christians took baptism a step further, associating it with Jesus' death and resurrection (see, for example, Romans 6:3, 4; 1 Peter 3:21).

1:5 Jesus came at a time in history when the entire civilized world was relatively peaceful under Roman rule, travel was easy, and there was a common language. The news about Jesus' life, death, and resurrection could spread quickly throughout the vast Roman Empire.

In Israel, people were ready for Jesus, too, and they flocked to hear this wilderness preacher. There had been no God-sent prophets for 400 years, since the days of Malachi (who wrote the last book of the Old Testament). Anticipation was growing that a great prophet, or the Messiah prophesied in the Old Testament, would soon come (see Luke 3:15).

• **1:5** The purpose of John's preaching was to prepare people to accept Jesus as God's Son. When John challenged the people to confess sin individually, he signaled the start of a new way to relate to God.

KEY PLACES IN MARK

The broken lines (—·—·) indicate modern boundaries.

Of the four Gospels, Mark's narrative is the most chronological—that is, most of the stories are positioned in the order they actually occurred. Though the shortest of the four, the Gospel of Mark contains the most events; it is action-packed. Most of this action centers in Galilee, where Jesus began his ministry. Capernaum served as his base of operation (1:21; 2:1; 9:33), from which he would go out to cities like Bethsaida, where he healed a blind man (8:22ff); Gennesaret, where he performed many healings (6:53ff); Tyre and Sidon (to the far north), where he healed many, drove out demons, and met the woman from Syrian Phoenicia (3:8; 7:24ff); and Caesarea Philippi, where Peter declared him to be the Messiah (8:27ff). After his ministry in Galilee and the surrounding regions, Jesus headed for Jerusalem (10:1). Before going there, Jesus told his disciples three times that he would be crucified there and then come back to life (8:31; 9:31; 10:33, 34).

Is change needed in your life before you can hear and understand Jesus' message? You have to admit that you need forgiveness before you can accept it. To prepare to receive Christ, repent. Turn away from the world's dead-end attractions, sinful temptations, and harmful attitudes, and turn to God. He can give you a new start.

1:6 John dressed much like the prophet Elijah (2 Kings 1:8) in order to distinguish himself from the religious leaders, whose flowing robes reflected their great pride in their position (12:38). John's striking appearance reinforced his striking message.

1:7, 8 Although John was the first genuine prophet in 400 years, Jesus the Messiah would be infinitely greater than he.

John was pointing out how insignificant he was compared to the one who was coming. John was not even worthy of being his slave. What John began, Jesus finished. What John prepared, Jesus fulfilled.

1:8 John said Jesus would baptize them with the Holy Spirit, sending the Holy Spirit to live within each believer. John's baptism with water prepared a person to receive Christ's message. This baptism demonstrated repentance, humility, and willingness to turn from sin. This was the *beginning* of the spiritual process. When Jesus baptizes with the Holy Spirit, the entire person is transformed by the Spirit's power. Jesus offers to us both forgiveness of sin and the power to live for him.

The Baptism of Jesus (**17**/Matthew 3:13-17; Luke 3:21-22)

1:11
Gen 22:2
Ps 2:7
Isa 42:1
Matt 12:18; 17:5
Mark 9:7
Luke 9:35
2 Pet 1:17

⁹One day Jesus came from Nazareth in Galilee, and John baptized him in the Jordan River. ¹⁰As Jesus came up out of the water, he saw the heavens splitting apart and the Holy Spirit descending on him* like a dove. ¹¹And a voice from heaven said, "You are my dearly loved Son, and you bring me great joy."

Satan Tempts Jesus in the Wilderness (**18**/Matthew 4:1-11; Luke 4:1-13)

¹²The Spirit then compelled Jesus to go into the wilderness, ¹³where he was tempted by Satan for forty days. He was out among the wild animals, and angels took care of him.

B. MESSAGE AND MINISTRY OF JESUS, THE SERVANT (1:14—13:37)

Mark tells us dramatic, action-packed stories. He gives us the most vivid account of Christ's activities. He features facts and actions, rather than teachings. The way Jesus lived his life is the perfect example of how we should live our lives today.

1. Jesus' ministry in Galilee

Jesus Preaches in Galilee (**30**/Matthew 4:12-17; Luke 4:14-15; John 4:43-45)

1:14
Mark 6:17-18
1:15
Gal 4:4
Eph 1:10

¹⁴Later on, after John was arrested, Jesus went into Galilee, where he preached God's Good News.* ¹⁵"The time promised by God has come at last!" he announced. "The Kingdom of God is near! Repent of your sins and believe the Good News!"

Four Fishermen Follow Jesus (**33**/Matthew 4:18-22)

¹⁶One day as Jesus was walking along the shore of the Sea of Galilee, he saw Simon* and his brother Andrew throwing a net into the water, for they fished for a living. ¹⁷Jesus called out to them, "Come, follow me, and I will show you how to fish for people!" ¹⁸And they left their nets at once and followed him.

1:10 Or *toward him,* or *into him.*   **1:14** Some manuscripts read *the Good News of the Kingdom of God.*   **1:16** *Simon* is called "Peter" in 3:16 and thereafter.

1:9 Jesus grew up in Nazareth, where he had lived since he was a young boy (Matthew 2:22, 23). Nazareth was a small town in Galilee, located about halfway between the Sea of Galilee and the Mediterranean Sea. The city was despised and avoided by many Jews (John 1:46). Nazareth was a crossroads for trade routes and had contact with many cultures.

1:9 If John's baptism was for repentance from sin, why was Jesus baptized? While even the greatest prophets (Isaiah, Jeremiah, Ezekiel) had to confess their sinfulness and need for repentance, Jesus didn't need to admit sin—he was sinless. Although Jesus didn't need forgiveness, he was baptized for the following reasons: (1) to begin his mission to bring the message of salvation to all people; (2) to show support for John's ministry; (3) to identify with our humanness and sin; (4) to give us an example to follow.

1:10, 11 The Spirit descended like a dove on Jesus, and the voice from heaven proclaimed the Father's approval of Jesus as his divine Son. Here we see all three members of the Trinity together—God the Father, God the Son, and God the Holy Spirit. (See also Matthew 28:19; Luke 1:35; John 15:26; 1 Corinthians 12:4-13; 2 Corinthians 13:14; Ephesians 2:18; 1 Thessalonians 1:2-5; 1 Peter 1:2.)

1:11 The dove and the voice from heaven were signs that Jesus was the Messiah. Many people want something tangible, visible, and "real" before they will believe. So Jesus did healings and other miracles, and God raised him from the dead. Still people doubt.

Will visible signs convince anyone? The "sign" that really brings us to faith is the power of God's message to answer the cry of the heart. To the confused, God offers a mind enlightened by faith. To the depressed, God offers a reason for joy. To the lonely, God offers eternal companionship. Don't look for a spectacular visible sign; instead, seek a cleansed and renewed life as evidence of his presence.

• **1:12, 13** Satan is an angel who rebelled against God. He is real, not symbolic, and is constantly working against God and those who obey him. Satan tempted Eve in the garden and persuaded her to sin; he tempted Jesus in the wilderness and did not persuade him to fall. To be tempted is not a sin. Tempting others or giving in to temptation *is* sin. For a more detailed account of Jesus' temptation, read Matthew 4:1-11.

1:12, 13 To identify fully with human beings, Jesus had to endure Satan's temptations. Although Jesus is God, he is also man. And as fully human, he was not exempt from Satan's attacks. Because Jesus faced temptations and overcame them, he can assist us in two important ways: (1) as an example of how to face temptation without sinning, and (2) as a helper who knows just what we need because he went through the same experience (Hebrews 4:15).

1:16-20 We often assume that Jesus' disciples were great men of faith from the first time they met Jesus. But they had to grow in their faith just as all believers do (14:48-50, 66-72; John 14:1-9; 20:26-29). This is apparently not the only time Jesus called Peter (Simon), James, and John to follow him (see Luke 5:1-11 and John 1:35-42 for two other times). Although it took time for Jesus' call and his message to get through, the disciples *followed.* In the same way, we may question and falter, but we must never stop following Jesus.

JESUS BEGINS HIS MINISTRY
When Jesus came from his home in Nazareth to begin his ministry, he first took two steps in preparation—baptism by John in the Jordan River and temptation by Satan in the rough Judean wilderness. After the temptations, Jesus returned to Galilee and later set up his home base in Capernaum.

Mediterranean Sea

N

GALILEE

Capernaum
Sea of Galilee
Nazareth
Jordan River
Aenon Salim

Bethany

Jerusalem
Dead Sea

JUDEA

0   20 Mi.
0   20 Km.

1:19
Matt 10:2
Mark 3:17; 10:35
Luke 5:10

19A little farther up the shore Jesus saw Zebedee's sons, James and John, in a boat repairing their nets. 20He called them at once, and they also followed him, leaving their father, Zebedee, in the boat with the hired men.

Jesus Teaches with Authority (34/Luke 4:31-37)

21Jesus and his companions went to the town of Capernaum. When the Sabbath day came,

1:22
Matt 7:28-29

he went into the synagogue and began to teach. 22The people were amazed at his teaching, for he taught with real authority—quite unlike the teachers of religious law.

23Suddenly, a man in the synagogue who was possessed by an evil* spirit began shouting,

1:24
Matt 8:29
John 6:69

24"Why are you interfering with us, Jesus of Nazareth? Have you come to destroy us? I know who you are—the Holy One of God!"

1:26
Mark 9:20

25Jesus cut him short. "Be quiet! Come out of the man," he ordered. 26At that, the evil spirit screamed, threw the man into a convulsion, and then came out of him.

27Amazement gripped the audience, and they began to discuss what had happened. "What sort of new teaching is this?" they asked excitedly. "It has such authority! Even evil spirits obey his orders!" 28The news about Jesus spread quickly throughout the entire region of Galilee.

Jesus Heals Peter's Mother-in-Law and Many Others (35/Matthew 8:14-17; Luke 4:38-41)

29After Jesus left the synagogue with James and John, they went to Simon and Andrew's home. 30Now Simon's mother-in-law was sick in bed with a high fever. They told Jesus about her right away. 31So he went to her bedside, took her by the hand, and helped her sit up. Then the fever left her, and she prepared a meal for them.

32That evening after sunset, many sick and demon-possessed people were brought to

1:23 Greek *unclean;* also in 1:26, 27.

• **1:17** Fishing was a major industry around the Sea of Galilee. Fishing with nets was the most common method. Jesus called the disciples to fish for people with the same energy they had used to fish for food. The gospel would be like a net, lifting people from dark waters into the light of day and transforming their lives. How can God use you to fish for people's souls? How can you train new converts to find new seas and cast new nets where waters have never been fished before? The gospel makes missionaries of all God's people. Where are you casting your net?

• **1:21** Jesus had recently moved to Capernaum from Nazareth (Matthew 4:12, 13). Capernaum was a thriving town with great wealth as well as great sin and decadence. Because it was the headquarters for many Roman troops, pagan influences from all over the Roman Empire were pervasive. This was an ideal place for Jesus to challenge both Jews and non-Jews with the Good News of God's Kingdom.

• **1:21, 22** Because the Temple in Jerusalem was too far for many Jews to travel to regularly for worship, many towns had synagogues serving both as places of worship and as schools. Beginning in the days of Ezra, about 450 B.C., a group of 10 Jewish families could start a synagogue. There, during the week, Jewish boys were taught the Old Testament law and Jewish religion. Girls could not attend. Each Saturday, the Sabbath, the Jewish men would gather to listen to a rabbi teach from the Scriptures. Because there was no permanent rabbi or teacher, it was customary for the synagogue leader to ask visiting teachers to speak. This is why Jesus often taught in the synagogues in the towns he visited. While the Jewish teachers often quoted from well-known rabbis to give their words more authority, Jesus didn't have that need. Because Jesus was God, he knew exactly what the Scriptures said and meant. He was the ultimate authority.

1:23 Evil spirits, or demons, are ruled by Satan. They work to tempt people to sin. They were not created by Satan because God is the Creator of all. Rather they are fallen angels who joined Satan in his rebellion. Though not all disease comes from Satan, demons can cause a person to become mute, deaf, blind, or insane. But in every case where demons confronted Jesus, they lost their power. Thus, God limits what evil spirits can do; they

can do nothing without his permission. During Jesus' life on earth, demons were allowed to be very active to demonstrate once and for all Christ's power and authority over them.

1:23ff Some people dismiss all accounts of demon possession as a primitive way to describe mental illness. Although throughout history mental illness has often been wrongly diagnosed as demon possession, clearly a hostile outside force controlled the man described here. Mark emphasized Jesus' conflict with evil powers to show his superiority over them, so he recorded many stories about Jesus driving out evil spirits. Jesus didn't have to conduct an elaborate exorcism ritual. His word was enough to send out the evil spirit.

• **1:23, 24** The evil spirit knew at once that Jesus was the Holy One sent from God. By including this event in his Gospel, Mark was establishing Jesus' credentials, showing that even the spiritual underworld recognized Jesus as the Messiah.

• **1:29-31** Each Gospel writer had a slightly different perspective as he wrote; thus, the comparable stories in the Gospels often highlight different details. In Matthew, Jesus touched the woman's hand. In Mark, he helped her up. In Luke, he spoke to the fever, and it left her. The accounts do not conflict. Just as four people might witness the same event and all recount different details, so each Gospel writer simply emphasized different details of this story.

• **1:32, 33** The people came to Jesus in the evening after sunset. That day had been the Sabbath (1:21), their day of rest, lasting from sunset Friday to sunset Saturday. The Jewish leaders had proclaimed that it was against the law to be healed on the Sabbath (Matthew 12:10; Luke 13:14). The people didn't want to break this law or the Jewish law that prohibited traveling on the Sabbath, so they waited until sunset. After the sun went down on Saturday, the crowds were free to find Jesus so he could heal them.

Jesus. ³³The whole town gathered at the door to watch. ³⁴So Jesus healed many people who were sick with various diseases, and he cast out many demons. But because the demons knew who he was, he did not allow them to speak.

1:34
Mark 3:12

Jesus Preaches throughout Galilee (36/Matthew 4:23-25; Luke 4:42-44)

³⁵Before daybreak the next morning, Jesus got up and went out to an isolated place to pray. ³⁶Later Simon and the others went out to find him. ³⁷When they found him, they said, "Everyone is looking for you."

³⁸But Jesus replied, "We must go on to other towns as well, and I will preach to them, too. That is why I came." ³⁹So he traveled throughout the region of Galilee, preaching in the synagogues and casting out demons.

1:38
Isa 61:1

1:39
Matt 4:23; 9:35

Jesus Heals a Man with Leprosy (38/Matthew 8:1-4; Luke 5:12-16)

⁴⁰A man with leprosy came and knelt in front of Jesus, begging to be healed. "If you are willing, you can heal me and make me clean," he said.

⁴¹Moved with compassion,* Jesus reached out and touched him. "I am willing," he said. "Be healed!" ⁴²Instantly the leprosy disappeared, and the man was healed. ⁴³Then Jesus sent him on his way with a stern warning: ⁴⁴"Don't tell anyone about this. Instead, go to the priest and let him examine you. Take along the offering required in the law of Moses for those who have been healed of leprosy.* This will be a public testimony that you have been cleansed."

1:44
Lev 14:1-32

⁴⁵But the man went and spread the word, proclaiming to everyone what had happened. As a result, large crowds soon surrounded Jesus, and he couldn't publicly enter a town anywhere. He had to stay out in the secluded places, but people from everywhere kept coming to him.

Jesus Heals a Paralyzed Man (39/Matthew 9:1-8; Luke 5:17-26)

2 When Jesus returned to Capernaum several days later, the news spread quickly that he was back home. ²Soon the house where he was staying was so packed with visitors that there was no more room, even outside the door. While he was preaching God's word to them, ³four men arrived carrying a paralyzed man on a mat. ⁴They couldn't bring him to

2:2
Eph 2:17
Heb 2:3

1:41 Some manuscripts read *Moved with anger.* **1:44** See Lev 14:2-32.

1:34 Why didn't Jesus want the demons to reveal who he was? (1) By commanding the demons to remain silent, Jesus proved his authority and power over them. (2) Jesus wanted the people to believe he was the Messiah because of what he said and did, not because of the demons' words. (3) Jesus wanted to reveal his identity as the Messiah according to his timetable, not according to Satan's timetable. Satan wanted the people to follow Jesus around for what they could get out of him, not because he was the Son of God who could truly set them free from sin's guilt and power.

● **1:35-37** Were the disciples impatient that Jesus prayed in solitude while so much ministry waited to be done? How would you have responded if you had been the one to find Jesus in prayer? It's easy to be so caught up with ministry that you neglect times of solitude, individual worship, and prayer. Perhaps you need to redesign your schedule to find time for earnest prayer. It is vitally important to: (1) seek the Lord before your busy schedule takes over your thoughts; (2) withdraw from noise and demands so you can focus on God; (3) take Jesus' attitude of regular communion with the Father; (4) reflect on the priorities Jesus had for his life; (5) determine to pray on a more regular basis, not just in times of crisis. If prayer was important for Jesus, then it must be important for his followers. Pray—even if you have to get up very early in the morning to do it!

● **1:39** The Romans divided the land of Israel into three separate regions: Galilee, Samaria, and Judea. Galilee was the northernmost region, an area about 60 miles long and 30 miles wide. Jesus did much of his ministry in this area, an ideal place for him to teach because there were over 250 towns concentrated there, with many synagogues.

● **1:40, 41** In keeping with the law in Leviticus 13 and 14, Jewish leaders declared people with leprosy unclean. This meant that lepers were unfit to participate in any religious or social activity. Because the law said that contact with any unclean person made a person unclean, too, some people even threw rocks at lepers to keep them at a safe distance. Even the mention of the name of this disabling disease terrified people. How astounding it was, then, when Jesus reached out and touched this man who had leprosy.

The real value of a person is inside, not outside. Although a person's body may be diseased or deformed, the person inside is no less valuable to God. In a sense, we are all people with leprosy because we have all been deformed by the ugliness of sin. By sending his Son, Jesus, God has touched us, giving us the opportunity to be healed.

1:43, 44 Although leprosy was incurable, many different types of skin diseases were classified together as "leprosy." According to the Old Testament laws about leprosy (Leviticus 13–14), when a leper was cured, he or she had to go to a priest to be examined. Then the leper was to give a thank offering at the Temple. Jesus adhered to these laws by sending the man to the priest, demonstrating Jesus' complete regard for God's law. Sending a healed leper to a priest was also a way to verify Jesus' great miracle to the community.

● **2:3** The paralyzed man's need moved his friends to action, and they brought him to Jesus. When you recognize someone's need, do you act? Many people have physical and spiritual needs you can meet, either by yourself or with others who are also concerned. Human need moved these four men; let it also move you to compassionate action.

2:4 The crowd that had gathered made it impossible to bring the paralyzed man close to Jesus. Successful churches or busy Christians can be oblivious to needy people who want to see

2:5
Luke 7:48

2:7
Ps 130:3-4
Isa 43:25

Jesus because of the crowd, so they dug a hole through the roof above his head. Then they lowered the man on his mat, right down in front of Jesus. ⁵Seeing their faith, Jesus said to the paralyzed man, "My child, your sins are forgiven."

⁶But some of the teachers of religious law who were sitting there thought to themselves, ⁷"What is he saying? This is blasphemy! Only God can forgive sins!"

PROMINENT JEWISH RELIGIOUS AND POLITICAL GROUPS	Name and Selected References	Description	Agreement with Jesus	Disagreement with Jesus
	PHARISEES Matthew 5:20 Matthew 23:1-36 Luke 6:2 Luke 7:36-47	Strict group of religious Jews who advocated obedience to the most minute portions of the Jewish law and traditions. Very influential in the synagogues.	Respect for the law, belief in the resurrection of the dead, committed to obeying God's will.	Rejected Jesus' claim to be Messiah because he did not follow all their traditions and associated with notoriously wicked people.
	SADDUCEES Matthew 3:7 Matthew 16:11, 12 Mark 12:18	Wealthy, upper class, Jewish priestly party. Rejected the authority of the Bible beyond the five books of Moses. Profited from business in the Temple. They, along with the Pharisees, were one of the two major parties of the Jewish high council.	Showed great respect for the five books of Moses, as well as the sanctity of the Temple.	Denied the resurrection of the dead. Thought the Temple could also be used as a place to transact business.
	TEACHERS OF RELIGIOUS LAW Matthew 7:29 Mark 2:6 Mark 2:16	Professional interpreters of the law—who especially emphasized the traditions. Many teachers of religious law were Pharisees.	Respect for the law. Committed to obeying God.	Denied Jesus' authority to reinterpret the law. Rejected Jesus as Messiah because he did not obey all of their traditions.
	SUPPORTERS OF HEROD Matthew 22:16 Mark 3:6 Mark 12:13	A Jewish political party of King Herod's supporters.	Unknown. In the Gospels they tried to trap Jesus with questions and plotted to kill him.	Afraid of Jesus causing political instability. They saw Jesus as a threat to their political future at a time when they were trying to regain from Rome some of their lost political power.
	ZEALOTS Luke 6:15 Acts 1:14	A fiercely dedicated group of Jewish patriots determined to end Roman rule in Israel.	Concerned about the future of Israel. Believed in the Messiah but did not recognize Jesus as the one sent by God.	Believed that the Messiah must be a political leader who would deliver Israel from Roman occupation.
	ESSENES none	Jewish monastic group practicing ritual purity and personal holiness.	Emphasized justice, honesty, commitment.	Believed ceremonial rituals made them righteous.

Jesus. In some churches, if the crowd is too thick and too disinterested, a needy person will simply wander away. How sad when the people in a church are so preoccupied with their own relationships and agendas that they don't even see those who are trying to get in. That should never happen. Where Jesus is present, may the faces of the faithful reflect his love, may their hands extend to greet all newcomers and seekers as friends, and may they open a way for others to come in.

• **2:4** Houses in Bible times were built of stone. They had flat roofs made of mud mixed with straw. Outside stairways led to the roofs. These friends may have carried the paralyzed man up the outside stairs to the roof. They then could easily have taken apart the mud and straw mixture to make a hole through which to lower their friend to Jesus.

2:6, 7 The teachers of religious law were in a perfect position, sitting where they could observe and criticize. Some sitting Christians follow their example. Is the music at church too fast or too loud? Is the sermon too long or too short? Do people aggravate you by sitting in your pew or dressing too casually? How much time do you spend worshiping in church and how much time do you spend complaining and criticizing? How about trying a little healthy activism—the kind that gets involved to work with fellow believers toward real progress on common goals, such as sharing the Good News, helping the needy, and building strong and caring disciples of Christ. Are you criticizing the church or changing the world?

8Jesus knew immediately what they were thinking, so he asked them, "Why do you question this in your hearts? 9Is it easier to say to the paralyzed man 'Your sins are forgiven,' or 'Stand up, pick up your mat, and walk'? 10So I will prove to you that the Son of Man* has the authority on earth to forgive sins." Then Jesus turned to the paralyzed man and said, 11"Stand up, pick up your mat, and go home!"

2:8
Matt 16:8

12And the man jumped up, grabbed his mat, and walked out through the stunned onlookers. They were all amazed and praised God, exclaiming, "We've never seen anything like this before!"

2:12
Matt 9:33

Jesus Eats with Sinners at Matthew's House (**40**/Matthew 9:9-13; Luke 5:27-32)

13Then Jesus went out to the lakeshore again and taught the crowds that were coming to him. 14As he walked along, he saw Levi son of Alphaeus sitting at his tax collector's booth. "Follow me and be my disciple," Jesus said to him. So Levi got up and followed him.

2:14
John 1:43

15Later, Levi invited Jesus and his disciples to his home as dinner guests, along with many tax collectors and other disreputable sinners. (There were many people of this kind among Jesus' followers.) 16But when the teachers of religious law who were Pharisees* saw him eating with tax collectors and other sinners, they asked his disciples, "Why does he eat with such scum?*"

17When Jesus heard this, he told them, "Healthy people don't need a doctor—sick people do. I have come to call not those who think they are righteous, but those who know they are sinners."

2:17
Luke 19:10
1 Tim 1:15

Religious Leaders Ask Jesus about Fasting (**41**/Matthew 9:14-17; Luke 5:33-39)

18Once when John's disciples and the Pharisees were fasting, some people came to Jesus and asked, "Why don't your disciples fast like John's disciples and the Pharisees do?"

19Jesus replied, "Do wedding guests fast while celebrating with the groom? Of course not. They can't fast while the groom is with them. 20But someday the groom will be taken away from them, and then they will fast.

2:19
John 3:29
Rev 19:7

2:20
Luke 17:22

21"Besides, who would patch old clothing with new cloth? For the new patch would shrink and rip away from the old cloth, leaving an even bigger tear than before.

2:10 "Son of Man" is a title Jesus used for himself.   **2:16a** Greek *the scribes of the Pharisees*.   **2:16b** Greek *with tax collectors and sinners?*

2:8-11 Before saying to the paralyzed man, "Stand up," Jesus said, "Your sins are forgiven." To the Jewish leaders this statement was blasphemous—claiming to do something only God could do. According to the law, the punishment for this sin was death (Leviticus 24:15, 16). The religious leaders understood correctly that Jesus was claiming divine prerogatives, but their judgment was wrong. Jesus was not blaspheming; his claim was true. Jesus is God, and he proved his claim by healing the paralyzed man (2:9-12).

2:10 This is the first time in Mark that Jesus is referred to as the "Son of Man," a title emphasizing that Jesus is fully human. The title, *Son of God* (see, for example, John 20:31) emphasizes that he is fully God. As God's Son, Jesus has the authority to forgive sin. As a man, he can identify with our deepest needs and sufferings and help us overcome sin (see also the note on 8:31).

2:14 Levi is another name for Matthew, the disciple who wrote the Gospel of Matthew. See Matthew's Profile in Matthew 9, p. 1557 for more information.

• **2:14** Capernaum (2:1) was a key military center for Roman troops as well as a thriving business community. Several major highways intersected in Capernaum, with merchants passing through from as far away as Egypt to the south and Mesopotamia to the north. Levi (Matthew), a Jew, worked for the Romans as the area's tax collector, collecting taxes from citizens as well as from merchants passing through town. Tax collectors were expected to take a commission on the taxes they collected. Most of them overcharged and vastly enriched themselves. Tax collectors were despised by the Jews because of their reputation for cheating and their support of Rome.

• **2:16, 17** The self-righteous Pharisees were indignant that Jesus would eat a meal with such sinners. But Jesus gladly associated

with sinners because he loved them and because he knew that they needed to hear what he had to say. Jesus spent time with whoever needed or wanted to hear his message—poor, rich, bad, good. We, too, must befriend those who need Christ, even if they do not seem to be ideal companions. Are there people you have been neglecting because of their reputation? They may be the ones who most need to see and hear the message of Christ's love in and from you.

• **2:18ff** John the Baptist had two goals: to lead people to repent of their sin, and to prepare them for Christ's coming. John's message was sobering, so he and his followers fasted. Fasting is both an outward sign of humility and regret for sin, and an inner discipline that clears the mind and keeps the spirit alert. Fasting empties the body of food; repentance empties the life of sin. Jesus' disciples did not need to fast to prepare for his coming because he was with them. Jesus did not condemn fasting, however. He himself fasted for 40 days (Matthew 4:2). Nevertheless, Jesus emphasized fasting with the right motives. The Pharisees fasted twice a week to show others how holy they were. Jesus explained that if people fast only to impress others, they will be twisting the purpose of fasting.

2:19 Jesus compared himself to a groom. In the Bible, the image of a bride is often used for God's people, and the image of a groom for the God who loves them (Isaiah 62:5; Matthew 25:1-13; Revelation 21:2).

2:21 Jesus did not come to patch up the old religious system of Judaism with its rules and traditions. His purpose was to fulfill it and start something new (though this "new" thing had been prophesied for centuries). Jesus Christ, God's Son, came to earth to offer all people forgiveness of sins and reconciliation with God. This new Good News did not fit into the old rigid legalistic system

2:22
Gal 3:1-3

22"And no one puts new wine into old wineskins. For the wine would burst the wine-skins, and the wine and the skins would both be lost. New wine calls for new wineskins."

The Disciples Pick Wheat on the Sabbath (**45**/Matthew 12:1-8; Luke 6:1-5)

2:23
Deut 23:25

23One Sabbath day as Jesus was walking through some grainfields, his disciples began breaking off heads of grain to eat. 24But the Pharisees said to Jesus, "Look, why are they breaking the law by harvesting grain on the Sabbath?"

2:25-26
1 Sam 21:1-7

25Jesus said to them, "Haven't you ever read in the Scriptures what David did when he and his companions were hungry? 26He went into the house of God (during the days when Abia-thar was high priest) and broke the law by eating the sacred loaves of bread that only the priests are allowed to eat. He also gave some to his companions."

2:27
Exod 23:12
Deut 5:14
John 7:21-24

27Then Jesus said to them, "The Sabbath was made to meet the needs of people, and not people to meet the requirements of the Sabbath. 28So the Son of Man is Lord, even over the Sabbath!"

Jesus Heals a Man's Hand on the Sabbath (**46**/Matthew 12:9-14; Luke 6:6-11)

3 Jesus went into the synagogue again and noticed a man with a deformed hand. 2Since it was the Sabbath, Jesus' enemies watched him closely. If he healed the man's hand, they planned to accuse him of working on the Sabbath.

3Jesus said to the man with the deformed hand, "Come and stand in front of everyone." 4Then he turned to his critics and asked, "Does the law permit good deeds on the Sabbath, or is it a day for doing evil? Is this a day to save life or to destroy it?" But they wouldn't answer him.

3:5
Mark 6:52; 8:17

5He looked around at them angrily and was deeply saddened by their hard hearts. Then he said to the man, "Hold out your hand." So the man held out his hand, and it was

---

of religion. It needed a fresh start. The message will always remain "new" because it must be accepted and applied in every generation. When you follow Christ, be prepared for new ways to live, new ways to look at people, and new ways to serve.

• **2:22** A wineskin was a goatskin sewed together at the edges to form a watertight bag. New wine, expanding as it aged, stretched the wineskin. New wine, therefore, could not be put into a wineskin that had already been stretched, or the taut skin would burst.

The Pharisees had become rigid like old wineskins. They could not accept faith in Jesus that would not be contained or limited by man-made ideas or rules. Your heart, like a wineskin, can become rigid and prevent you from accepting the new life that Christ offers. Keep your heart pliable and open to accepting the life-changing truths of Christ.

• **2:23** Jesus and his disciples were not stealing when they picked the grain. Leviticus 19:9, 10 and Deuteronomy 23:25 say that farmers were to leave the edges of their fields unharvested so that some of their crops could be picked by travelers and by the poor. Just as walking on a sidewalk is not trespassing on private prop-erty, picking heads of grain at the edge of a field was not stealing.

• **2:24** God's law said that crops should not be harvested on the Sabbath (Exodus 34:21). This law prevented farmers from becoming greedy and ignoring God on the Sabbath. It also protected laborers from being overworked.

The Pharisees interpreted the action of Jesus and his disci-ples—picking the grain and eating it as they walked through the fields—as harvesting; and so they judged Jesus a lawbreaker. But Jesus and the disciples clearly were not harvesting the grain for personal gain; they were simply looking for something to eat. The Pharisees were so focused on the words of the rule that they missed its intent.

2:25-28 Jesus used the example of David to point out how ridiculous the Pharisees' accusations were (this incident occurred in 1 Samuel 21:1-6). God created the Sabbath for our benefit; we are restored both physically and spiritually when we take time to rest and to focus on God. For the Phari-sees, Sabbath rules had become more important than Sabbath rest. Both David and Jesus understood that the intent of God's law is to promote love for God and others.

The Christian faith involves many rules that are meant to be

governed by love. That makes love the highest rule, but it also moves Christians toward personal sacrifice, discipline, and responsibility—scarce resources in today's world. When con-fronted with rules of your own or others' making, ask: (1) Does the rule serve God's purposes? (2) Does the rule reveal God's character? (3) Does the rule help people get into God's family, or keep them out? (4) Does the rule have biblical roots that can be supported in the context of all of Scripture? Good rules pass all four tests.

2:26 The "sacred loaves of bread" (called the Bread of the Presence) were set before God on a table in the Holy Place in the Tabernacle (and later in the Temple). Every Sabbath, 12 freshly-baked loaves of bread were set out, and the priests ate the old loaves. See Exodus 25:30 and Leviticus 24:5-9 for more about the Bread of the Presence.

3:2 Already many of the religious leaders had turned against Jesus and become his "enemies." They were jealous of his popularity, his miracles, and the authority in his teaching and actions. They valued their status in the community and their opportunity for personal gain so much that they lost sight of their goal as religious leaders—to point people toward God. Of all people, the Pharisees should have recognized the Messiah, but they refused to acknowledge him because they were not will-ing to give up their treasured position and power. When Jesus exposed their attitudes, he became their enemy instead of their Messiah, and they began looking for ways to turn the people against him.

3:5 Jesus was angry about the Pharisees' uncaring attitudes. Anger itself is not wrong. It depends on what makes us angry and what we do with our anger. Too often we express our anger in selfish and harmful ways. By contrast, Jesus expressed his anger by correcting a problem—healing the man's hand. Use your anger to find constructive solutions rather than to tear people down.

THE TWELVE

Name	Occupation	Outstanding Characteristics	Major Events in His Life
SIMON PETER (son of John)	Fisherman	Impulsive; later—bold in preaching about Jesus	One of three in core group of disciples; recognized Jesus as the Messiah; denied Christ and repented; preached Pentecost sermon; a leader of the Jerusalem church; baptized Gentiles; wrote 1 and 2 Peter.
JAMES (son of Zebedee), he and his brother, John, were called the "Sons of Thunder"	Fisherman	Ambitious, short-tempered, judgmental, deeply committed to Jesus	Also in core group; he and his brother, John, asked Jesus for places of honor in his Kingdom; wanted to call fire down to destroy a Samaritan village; first disciple to be martyred.
JOHN (son of Zebedee), James's brother, and "the disciple Jesus loved"	Fisherman	Ambitious, judgmental, later—very loving	Third disciple in core group; asked Jesus for a place of honor in his Kingdom; wanted to call down fire on a Samaritan village; a leader of the Jerusalem church; wrote the Gospel of John, 1, 2, 3 John, and Revelation.
ANDREW (Peter's brother)	Fisherman	Eager to bring others to Jesus	Accepted John the Baptist's testimony about Jesus; told Peter about Jesus; he and Philip told Jesus that Greeks wanted to see him.
PHILIP	Fisherman	Questioning attitude	Told Nathanael about Jesus; wondered how Jesus could feed the 5,000; asked Jesus to show his followers God the Father; he and Andrew told Jesus that Greeks wanted to see him.
NATHANAEL	Unknown	Honest and straightforward	Initially rejected Jesus because Jesus was from Nazareth but acknowledged him as the "Son of God" and "King of Israel" when they met.
MATTHEW (Levi)	Tax collector	Despised outcast because of his dishonest career	Abandoned his corrupt (and financially profitable) way of life to follow Jesus; invited Jesus to a party with his notorious friends; wrote the Gospel of Matthew.
THOMAS (the Twin)	Unknown	Courage and doubt	Suggested the disciples go with Jesus to Bethany—even if it meant death; asked Jesus about where he was going; refused to believe Jesus was risen until he could see Jesus alive and touch his wounds.
JAMES (son of Alphaeus)	Unknown	Unknown	Became one of Jesus' disciples.
THADDAEUS (Judas son of James)	Unknown	Unknown	Asked Jesus why he would reveal himself to his followers and not to the world.
SIMON THE ZEALOT	Unknown	Fierce patriotism	Became a disciple of Jesus.
JUDAS ISCARIOT	Unknown	Treacherous and greedy	Became one of Jesus' disciples; betrayed Jesus; committed suicide.

Jesus' faithful disciples were ordinary men who became extraordinary because of Jesus Christ. Despite their confusion and lack of understanding during his lifetime, they became powerful witnesses to his resurrection. Their lives were transformed by God's power. The story of Jesus' disciples does not end with the Gospels. It continues in the book of Acts and many of the letters.

DISCIPLES

What Jesus Said about Him	*A Key Lesson from His Life*	*Selected References*
Named him Peter, "rock"; called him "Satan" when he urged Jesus to reject the cross; said he would fish for people; he received revelation from God; he would deny Jesus; he would later be crucified for his faith.	Christians falter at times, but when they return to Jesus, he forgives them and strengthens their faith	Matthew 4:18-20 Mark 8:29-33 Luke 22:31-34 John 21:15-19 Acts 2:14-41 Acts 10:1–11:18
Called James and John "Sons of Thunder"; said he would fish for people; would drink the cup Jesus drank.	Christians must be willing to die for Jesus.	Mark 3:17 Mark 10:35-40 Luke 9:52-56 Acts 12:1, 2
Called John and James "Sons of Thunder"; said he would fish for people; would drink the cup Jesus drank; would take care of Jesus' mother after Jesus' death.	The transforming power of the love of Christ is available to all.	Mark 1:19 Mark 10:35-40 Luke 9:52-56 John 19:26, 27 John 21:20-24
Said he would fish for people.	Christians are to tell other people about Jesus.	Matthew 4:18-20 John 1:35-42; 6:8, 9 John 12:20-24
Asked if Philip realized that to know and see him was to know and see the Father.	God uses our questions to teach us.	Matthew 10:3 John 1:43-46; 6:2-7 John 12:20-22 John 14:8-11
Called him "a true son of Israel" and "an honest man."	Jesus respects honesty in people—even if they challenge him because of it.	Mark 3:18 John 1:45-51 John 21:1-13
Called him to be a disciple.	Christianity is not for people who think they're already good; it is for people who know they've failed and want help.	Matthew 9:9-13 Mark 2:15-17 Luke 5:27-32
Said Thomas believed because he actually saw Jesus after the Resurrection.	Even when Christians experience serious doubts, Jesus reaches out to them to restore their faith.	Matthew 10:3 John 14:5; 20:24-29 John 21:1-13
Unknown	Unknown	Matthew 10:3 Mark 3:18 Luke 6:15
Unknown	Christians follow Jesus because they believe in him; they do not always understand the details of God's plan.	Matthew 10:3 Mark 3:18 John 14:22
Unknown	If we are willing to give up our plans for the future, we can participate in Jesus' plans.	Matthew 10:4 Mark 3:18 Luke 6:15
Called him "a devil"; said Judas would betray Jesus.	It is not enough to be familiar with Jesus' teachings. Jesus' true followers love and obey him.	Matthew 26:20-25 Luke 22:47, 48 John 12:4-8

restored! 6At once the Pharisees went away and met with the supporters of Herod to plot how to kill Jesus.

3:6
Matt 22:15-16
Mark 12:13

Large Crowds Follow Jesus (47/Matthew 12:15-21)

7Jesus went out to the lake with his disciples, and a large crowd followed him. They came from all over Galilee, Judea, 8Jerusalem, Idumea, from east of the Jordan River, and even from as far north as Tyre and Sidon. The news about his miracles had spread far and wide, and vast numbers of people came to see him.

3:7-8
Matt 4:25

9Jesus instructed his disciples to have a boat ready so the crowd would not crush him. 10He had healed many people that day, so all the sick people eagerly pushed forward to touch him. 11And whenever those possessed by evil* spirits caught sight of him, the spirits would throw them to the ground in front of him shrieking, "You are the Son of God!" 12But Jesus sternly commanded the spirits not to reveal who he was.

3:10
Mark 4:1
3:11-12
Mark 1:24-25, 34
Luke 4:41
Acts 16:16-17

Jesus Chooses the Twelve Disciples (48/Luke 6:12-16)

13Afterward Jesus went up on a mountain and called out the ones he wanted to go with him. And they came to him. 14Then he appointed twelve of them and called them his apostles.* They were to accompany him, and he would send them out to preach, 15giving them authority to cast out demons. 16These are the twelve he chose:

3:14
Mark 6:30
3:16
Matt 16:17-18
John 1:42

Simon (whom he named Peter),

17 James and John (the sons of Zebedee, but Jesus nicknamed them "Sons of Thunder"*),

3:17
Luke 9:54

18 Andrew,

Philip,

Bartholomew,

Matthew,

Thomas,

James (son of Alphaeus),

Thaddaeus,

Simon (the zealot*),

19 Judas Iscariot (who later betrayed him).

3:11 Greek *unclean;* also in 3:30.   3:14 Some manuscripts do not include *and called them his apostles.*
3:17 Greek *whom he named Boanerges, which means Sons of Thunder.*   3:18 Greek *the Cananean,* an Aramaic term for Jewish nationalists.

• **3:6** The Pharisees were a Jewish religious group that zealously followed the Old Testament laws as well as their own religious traditions. They were highly respected in the community, but they hated Jesus because he challenged their proud attitudes and dishonorable motives.

The supporters of Herod were a Jewish political party that hoped to restore Herod the Great's line to the throne. Jesus was a threat to them as well because he challenged their political ambitions. These two groups were normally at odds, but they joined forces against Jesus.

3:6 The Pharisees had accused Jesus of breaking their law that said medical attention could be given to no one on the Sabbath except in matters of life and death. Ironically, the Pharisees themselves were breaking God's law by plotting murder.

• **3:7-11** The evil spirits knew that Jesus was the Son of God, but they had no intention of following him. Many people followed Jesus but didn't understand his true purpose for coming. Some people came for miracles, some came to hear his teaching, but they didn't understand the way of the cross. Knowing about Jesus, or even believing that he is God's Son, does not guarantee salvation. You must also follow and obey him (see James 2:17).

3:12 Jesus warned the evil spirits not to reveal his identity because he did not want them to reinforce a popular misconception. The huge crowds were looking for a political and military leader who would free them from Rome's control, and they thought that the Messiah predicted by the Old Testament prophets would be this kind of man. Jesus wanted to teach the people about the kind of Messiah he really was—one who was far different from their expectations. Christ's Kingdom is spiritual. It begins with the overthrow of sin in people's hearts, not with the overthrow of governments.

3:13 What does it mean to hear the "call" of God? First, God calls you to faith in Jesus. You will know this call by the growing desire in your heart to settle the matter of peace with God speedily. Respond to him—answer with a grateful, "Yes, Lord, I need you!"

Second, God calls you to service in Jesus' name. Wherever you are (and sometimes you need to move), whatever you're doing (and sometimes you need to upgrade your skills), God has a place of service for you. Jesus calls you and he wants you. Answer this call thoughtfully, seriously, in consultation with other Christians, saying, "Yes, Lord, I love you and will follow you!"

• **3:14** From the hundreds of people who followed him from place to place, Jesus chose 12 to be his *apostles. Apostle* means "messenger or authorized representative." Why did Jesus choose 12 disciples? The number 12 corresponds to the 12 tribes of Israel (Matthew 19:28), showing the continuity between the old religious system and the new one based on Jesus' message. Many people followed Jesus, but these 12 received the most intense training.

Jesus did not choose these 12 to be his associates and companions because of their faith; their faith often faltered. He didn't choose them because of their talent and ability; no one stood out with unusual ability. The disciples represented a wide range of backgrounds and life experiences, but apparently they had no more leadership potential than those who were not chosen. The one characteristic they all shared was their willingness to obey Jesus. After Jesus' ascension, they were filled with the Holy Spirit and empowered to carry out special roles in the growth of the early church. We should not disqualify ourselves from service to Christ because we do not have the expected credentials. Being a good disciple is simply a matter of following Jesus with a willing heart.

Religious Leaders Accuse Jesus of Getting His Power from Satan (**74**/Matthew 12:22-37)

20One time Jesus entered a house, and the crowds began to gather again. Soon he and his disciples couldn't even find time to eat. 21When his family heard what was happening, they tried to take him away. "He's out of his mind," they said.

22But the teachers of religious law who had arrived from Jerusalem said, "He's possessed by Satan,* the prince of demons. That's where he gets the power to cast out demons."

23Jesus called them over and responded with an illustration. "How can Satan cast out Satan?" he asked. 24"A kingdom divided by civil war will collapse. 25Similarly, a family splintered by feuding will fall apart. 26And if Satan is divided and fights against himself, how can he stand? He would never survive. 27Let me illustrate this further. Who is powerful enough to enter the house of a strong man like Satan and plunder his goods? Only someone even stronger—someone who could tie him up and then plunder his house.

28"I tell you the truth, all sin and blasphemy can be forgiven, 29but anyone who blasphemes the Holy Spirit will never be forgiven. This is a sin with eternal consequences." 30He told them this because they were saying, "He's possessed by an evil spirit."

Jesus Describes His True Family (**76**/Matthew 12:46-50; Luke 8:19-21)

31Then Jesus' mother and brothers came to see him. They stood outside and sent word for him to come out and talk with them. 32There was a crowd sitting around Jesus, and someone said, "Your mother and your brothers* are outside asking for you."

33Jesus replied, "Who is my mother? Who are my brothers?" 34Then he looked at those around him and said, "Look, these are my mother and brothers. 35Anyone who does God's will is my brother and sister and mother."

3:22 John 7:20; 8:48, 52; 10:20

3:27 Isa 49:24-25

3:28-30 Luke 12:10 1 Jn 5:16

3:31 Mark 6:3 John 7:3-5

3:34 John 20:17 Rom 8:29 Heb 2:11

3:22 Greek *Beelzeboul;* other manuscripts read *Beezeboul;* Latin version reads *Beelzebub.* **3:32** Some manuscripts add *and sisters.*

• **3:21** With the crowds pressing in on him, Jesus didn't even take time to eat. Because of this, his friends and family came to take charge of him (3:31, 32), thinking he had gone "over the edge" as a religious fanatic. They were concerned for him, but they missed the point of his ministry. Even those who were closest to Jesus were slow to understand who he was and what he had come to do.

3:21 The family may be the most difficult place to be a witness for Jesus. To be the first or only Christian may go against the grain. Your faith may be misinterpreted as criticism. Your zeal may be misunderstood. You may be accused of being a hypocrite because other areas of your life still fall short of Christ's ideals. Uncommitted people may view your new commitment to the Bible as unreasonable bigotry.

Family members require the most patience. They see you at your worst when your guard is down. Remember that Christ's family rejected and ridiculed him. Jesus knows what you face by trying to be a witness for him in your own family. Stay true to your faith. Don't respond negatively to the attacks that may come. Over time, your love for your family will have a positive effect.

3:22-27 These teachers of the law brought a nonsensical accusation against Jesus. They tried to say that Jesus was driving out demons by the power of the prince of demons—in other words, that Jesus' power came from Satan, not God. They wanted the people to believe that Jesus himself was possessed (3:30). This would disprove his claim as the Messiah and place him instead in league with the devil.

The more effective you are in your Christian life, the more extreme will be the attacks of the enemy. Even the most ridiculous accusation will convince some when it's cleverly packaged to sound sincere and concerned. Stand firm for the truth, even when clever attacks come.

3:27 Although God permits Satan to work in our world, God is still in control. Because he is God, Jesus has power over Satan and is able to drive out demons, thus ending their terrible work in people's lives. One day Satan will be bound forever (Revelation 20:10).

3:28, 29 Christians sometimes wonder if they have committed this sin of blaspheming the Holy Spirit. Christians need not worry because this sin is attributing to the devil the work of the Holy Spirit. It reveals a heart attitude of unbelief and unrepentance. Deliberate, ongoing rejection of the work of the Holy Spirit is blasphemy because it is rejecting God himself. The religious leaders accused Jesus of blasphemy, but ironically they were the guilty ones when they looked Jesus in the face and accused him of being possessed by Satan.

• **3:31-35** Jesus' mother was Mary (Luke 1:30, 31), and his brothers were probably the other children Mary and Joseph had after Jesus (see also 6:3). Some Christians believe the ancient tradition that Jesus was Mary's only child. If this is true, the "brothers" were possibly cousins (cousins were often called brothers in those days). Some have offered yet another suggestion: When Joseph married Mary, he was a widower, and these were his children by his first marriage. Most likely, however, these were Jesus' half brothers (see Mark 6:3, 4).

Jesus' family did not yet fully understand his ministry, as can be seen in 3:21. Jesus explained that in our spiritual family, the relationships are ultimately more important and longer lasting than those formed in our physical families.

3:33-35 God's family is accepting and doesn't exclude anyone. Although Jesus cared for his mother and brothers, he also cared for all those who loved him. Jesus did not show partiality; he allowed everyone the privilege of obeying God and becoming part of his family. In our increasingly computerized, impersonal world, warm relationships among members of God's family take on major importance. The church should give the loving, personalized care that many people find nowhere else.

Jesus Tells the Parable of the Four Soils (**77**/Matthew 13:1-9; Luke 8:4-8)

4 Once again Jesus began teaching by the lakeshore. A very large crowd soon gathered around him, so he got into a boat. Then he sat in the boat while all the people remained on the shore. ²He taught them by telling many stories in the form of parables, such as this one:

4:2
Mark 4:33-34

³"Listen! A farmer went out to plant some seed. ⁴As he scattered it across his field, some of the seed fell on a footpath, and the birds came and ate it. ⁵Other seed fell on shallow soil with underlying rock. The seed sprouted quickly because the soil was shallow. ⁶But the plant soon wilted under the hot sun, and since it didn't have deep roots, it died. ⁷Other seed fell among thorns that grew up and choked out the tender plants so they produced no grain. ⁸Still other seeds fell on fertile soil, and they sprouted, grew, and produced a crop that was thirty, sixty, and even a hundred times as much as had been planted!" ⁹Then he said, "Anyone with ears to hear should listen and understand."

4:9
Matt 11:15
Mark 4:23

Jesus Explains the Parable of the Four Soils (**78**/Matthew 13:10-23; Luke 8:9-18)

¹⁰Later, when Jesus was alone with the twelve disciples and with the others who were gathered around, they asked him what the parables meant.

¹¹He replied, "You are permitted to understand the secret* of the Kingdom of God. But I use parables for everything I say to outsiders, ¹²so that the Scriptures might be fulfilled:

4:12
†Isa 6:9-10
John 12:39-40
Acts 28:26-27

'When they see what I do,
  they will learn nothing.
When they hear what I say,
  they will not understand.
Otherwise, they will turn to me
  and be forgiven.'*"

¹³Then Jesus said to them, "If you can't understand the meaning of this parable, how will you understand all the other parables? ¹⁴The farmer plants seed by taking God's word to others. ¹⁵The seed that fell on the footpath represents those who hear the message, only to have Satan come at once and take it away. ¹⁶The seed on the rocky soil represents those who hear the message and immediately receive it with joy. ¹⁷But since they don't have deep roots, they don't last long. They fall away as soon as they have problems or are persecuted for believing God's word. ¹⁸The seed that fell among the thorns represents others who hear God's word, ¹⁹but all too quickly the message is crowded out by the worries of this life, the

4:14
Eph 3:8
Jas 1:18
1 Pet 1:23-25

4:15
2 Cor 4:4
1 Pet 5:8

4:19
1 Tim 6:9-10, 17
1 Jn 2:15-17

4:11 Greek *mystery.*   **4:12** Isa 6:9-10 (Greek version).

- **4:2** Jesus taught the people by telling stories called parables, using familiar scenes to explain spiritual truths. This method of teaching compels the listener to think. It conceals the truth from those who are too stubborn or prejudiced to hear what is being taught. Most parables have one main point, so we must be careful not to go beyond what Jesus intended to teach.

- **4:3** Seed was planted by hand. As the farmer walked across the field, he threw handfuls of seed onto the ground from a large bag slung across his shoulders. The plants did not grow in neat rows as they do with today's machine planting. No matter how skillful, no farmer could keep some of his seed from falling on the footpath, from being scattered among rocks and thorns, or from being carried off by the wind. So the farmer would throw the seed liberally, and enough would fall on good ground to ensure the harvest.

- **4:9** The hearing Jesus wants from us is not the kind we use when we listen to background music or when someone starts to recount a long story we've already heard. To truly "hear" Jesus' words is to believe them, to use them immediately in decisions and attitudes, and to base life on them—your recreation and work, family plans and money matters, praying and singing. To hear Jesus' words is to make Jesus your true Lord. What is Jesus saying to you?

4:14-20 This parable should encourage spiritual "sowers"— those who teach, preach, and lead others. The farmer sowed good seed, but not all the seed sprouted, and even the plants that grew had varying yields. Don't be discouraged if you do not always see results as you faithfully teach the Word. Some people do not understand God's truth because they are not ready for it. God reveals truth to people who will act on it and make it visible in their lives. When you talk with people about God, be aware that they will not understand if they are not yet ready. Be patient, taking every chance to tell them more about God and praying that the Holy Spirit will open their minds and hearts to receive the truth and act on it. Productivity is in God's hands.

- **4:14-20** The four soils represent four different ways people respond to God's message. Usually we think that Jesus was talking about four different kinds of people. But he may also have been talking about (1) different times or phases in a person's life or (2) how we willingly apply God's message to some areas of our life but resist applying it to others. For example, you may be open to God about your future but closed concerning how you spend your money. You may respond like good soil to God's demand for worship but respond like rocky soil to his demand to give to people in need. Strive to be like good soil in every area of your life at all times.

4:19 Worries of this life, the lure of wealth, and the desire for things plagued first-century disciples just as they do us today. How easy it is for our daily routines to become overcrowded. A life packed with materialistic pursuits crowds out God's Word and leaves us unfruitful for him. Stay free so you can hear God when he speaks.

lure of wealth, and the desire for other things, so no fruit is produced. 20 And the seed that fell on good soil represents those who hear and accept God's word and produce a harvest of thirty, sixty, or even a hundred times as much as had been planted!"

4:21-25
Matt 5:15

4:22
Matt 10:26
Luke 12:2

4:23
Matt 11:15; 13:43

4:25
Matt 13:12; 25:29
Luke 19:26

21 Then Jesus asked them, "Would anyone light a lamp and then put it under a basket or under a bed? Of course not! A lamp is placed on a stand, where its light will shine. 22 For everything that is hidden will eventually be brought into the open, and every secret will be brought to light. 23 Anyone with ears to hear should listen and understand."

24 Then he added, "Pay close attention to what you hear. The closer you listen, the more understanding you will be given*—and you will receive even more. 25 To those who listen to my teaching, more understanding will be given. But for those who are not listening, even what little understanding they have will be taken away from them."

Jesus Tells the Parable of the Growing Seed (**79**)

4:26-27
1 Cor 3:6-7

4:28-29
Matt 9:37-38
Rev 14:15

26 Jesus also said, "The Kingdom of God is like a farmer who scatters seed on the ground. 27 Night and day, while he's asleep or awake, the seed sprouts and grows, but he does not understand how it happens. 28 The earth produces the crops on its own. First a leaf blade pushes through, then the heads of wheat are formed, and finally the grain ripens. 29 And as soon as the grain is ready, the farmer comes and harvests it with a sickle, for the harvest time has come."

Jesus Tells the Parable of the Mustard Seed (**81**/Matthew 13:31-32)

4:32
Ezek 17:23; 31:6
Dan 4:12, 21

4:33
Matt 13:34-35

4:34
John 16:25

30 Jesus said, "How can I describe the Kingdom of God? What story should I use to illustrate it? 31 It is like a mustard seed planted in the ground. It is the smallest of all seeds, 32 but it becomes the largest of all garden plants; it grows long branches, and birds can make nests in its shade."

33 Jesus used many similar stories and illustrations to teach the people as much as they could understand. 34 In fact, in his public ministry he never taught without using parables; but afterward, when he was alone with his disciples, he explained everything to them.

Jesus Calms the Storm (**87**/Matthew 8:23-27; Luke 8:22-25)

35 As evening came, Jesus said to his disciples, "Let's cross to the other side of the lake." 36 So they took Jesus in the boat and started out, leaving the crowds behind (although other boats followed). 37 But soon a fierce storm came up. High waves were breaking into the boat, and it began to fill with water.

38 Jesus was sleeping at the back of the boat with his head on a cushion. The disciples woke him up, shouting, "Teacher, don't you care that we're going to drown?"

4:24 Or *The measure you give will be the measure you get back.*

4:21 Many Christians today are hidden from sight, reluctant to be identified as Christians. Such a Christian is like a brand-new light that never leaves the carton it came in. If a lamp doesn't help people see, it isn't worth much. Does your life show other people how to find God and how to live for him? If not, ask what "baskets" have hidden your light. Complacency, resentment, embarrassment, stubbornness of heart, or disobedience could keep you from shining. What do you need to do to let your light shine?

• **4:24, 25** The light of Jesus' truth is revealed to us, not hidden. But we may not be able to see or to use all of that truth right now. Only as we put God's teachings into practice will we understand and see more of the truth. The truth is clear, but our ability to understand is imperfect. As we obey, we will sharpen our vision and increase our understanding (see James 1:22-25).

4:25 Jesus' words may have been directed to the Jews who had no understanding of Jesus and would lose even what they had—their privileged status as God's people. Or Jesus might have meant that when people reject him, their hardness of heart drives away or renders useless even the little understanding they had; thus, any opportunity to share in God's Kingdom will eventually be taken away completely. To understand Jesus' message, people must listen and respond. Those who listen casually, for whatever reason, will miss the point.

4:26-29 God promises that his harvest will be magnificent and prolific—the best fruit ever grown. Your witness may be weak and your efforts may seem to influence so few, but the Word of God is a powerful growth agent. Keep your eyes on the great harvest to come and don't let bad soil or weeds discourage you from faithful service and witness.

4:30-32 Jesus used this parable to explain that although Christianity had very small beginnings, it would grow into a worldwide community of believers. When you feel alone in your stand for Christ, realize that God is building a worldwide Kingdom. He has faithful followers in every part of the world. Your faith, no matter how small, can join with that of others to accomplish great things.

4:35-38 The "lake" is the Sea of Galilee, a body of water 680 feet below sea level and surrounded by hills. Winds blowing across the land intensify close to the sea, often causing violent and unexpected storms. The disciples were seasoned fishermen, who had spent their lives fishing on this huge lake, but during this squall they panicked.

4:37 Problems occur in every area of life. The disciples needed rest, but they encountered a terrible storm. The Christian life may have more stormy weather than calm seas. As Christ's follower, be prepared for the storms that will surely come. Do not surrender to the stress, but remain resilient and recover from setbacks. With faith in Christ, you can pray, trust, and move ahead. When a squall approaches, lean into the wind and trust God.

³⁹When Jesus woke up, he rebuked the wind and said to the waves, "Silence! Be still!" **4:39** Pss 65:8; Suddenly the wind stopped, and there was a great calm. ⁴⁰Then he asked them, "Why are 107:25-32 you afraid? Do you still have no faith?"

⁴¹The disciples were absolutely terrified. "Who is this man?" they asked each other. **4:41** Ps 33:8-9 "Even the wind and waves obey him!"

Jesus Sends Demons into a Herd of Pigs (88/Matthew 8:28-34; Luke 8:26-39)

5 So they arrived at the other side of the lake, in the region of the Gerasenes.* ²When Jesus climbed out of the boat, a man possessed by an evil* spirit came out from a cemetery to meet him. ³This man lived among the burial caves and could no longer be restrained, even with a chain. ⁴Whenever he was put into chains and shackles—as he often was—he snapped the chains from his wrists and smashed the shackles. No one was strong enough to subdue him. ⁵Day and night he wandered among the burial caves and in the hills, howling and cutting himself with sharp stones.

⁶When Jesus was still some distance away, the man saw him, ran to meet him, and bowed low before him. ⁷With a shriek, he screamed, "Why are you interfering with me, Jesus, Son **5:7-8** of the Most High God? In the name of God, I beg you, don't torture me!" ⁸For Jesus had Acts 16:17 already said to the spirit, "Come out of the man, you evil spirit."

⁹Then Jesus demanded, "What is your name?"

And he replied, "My name is Legion, because there are many of us inside this man." ¹⁰Then the evil spirits begged him again and again not to send them to some distant place.

¹¹There happened to be a large herd of pigs feeding on the hillside nearby. ¹²"Send us into those pigs," the spirits begged. "Let us enter them."

¹³So Jesus gave them permission. The evil spirits came out of the man and entered the pigs, and the entire herd of about 2,000 pigs plunged down the steep hillside into the lake and drowned in the water.

5:1 Other manuscripts read *Gadarenes;* still others read *Gergesenes.* See Matt 8:28; Luke 8:26.   **5:2** Greek *unclean;* also in 5:8, 13.

4:41 The disciples lived with Jesus, but they underestimated him. They did not see that his power applied to their very own situation. Jesus has been with his people for 20 centuries, and yet we, like the disciples, underestimate his power to handle crises in our lives. The disciples did not yet know enough about Jesus. We cannot make the same excuse.

5:1, 2 Although we cannot be sure why demon possession occurs, we know that evil spirits can use the human body to distort and destroy people's relationship with God and likeness to him. Even today, demons are dangerous, powerful, and destructive. While it is important to recognize their evil activity, we should avoid any curiosity about or involvement with demonic forces or the occult (Deuteronomy 18:10-12). If we resist the devil and his influences, he will flee from us (James 4:7).

5:7 The demon screamed at Jesus, "Why are you interfering with me?" It was a shriek of fear, defense, and rebellion against God. No one today would like to admit to being demon possessed, but most of our society, like the demon, is screaming at God, the church, and Christian values, "Why are you interfering with me? Get out of my life!" When people reject Jesus Christ and his authority, they put themselves on the side of the demons and are heading in the same direction. Every person must ask: Will I choose autonomy and self-will leading to destruction, or will I choose Christ's loving leadership over my life, giving me forgiveness, healing from sin, cleansing, and true freedom? The answer has eternal implications.

5:9 The evil spirit said its name was Legion. A legion was the largest unit of the Roman army, consisting of 3,000 to 6,000 soldiers. This man was possessed by many demons.

5:10 Mark often highlights the supernatural struggle between Jesus and Satan. The demons' goal was to control the humans they inhabited; Jesus' goal was to give people freedom from sin and Satan's control. The demons knew they had no power over Jesus, so they simply begged not to be sent to some distant place ("the bottomless pit" in Luke 8:31). Jesus granted their request to enter into the herd of pigs (5:13), but ended their destructive work in people. Perhaps Jesus let the demons destroy the pigs to demonstrate his own superiority over a very powerful yet destructive force. He could have sent them to hell, but he did not because the time for judgment had not yet come. In the end, the devil and all his demons will be sent into eternal fire (Matthew 25:41).

HEALING A DEMON-POSSESSED MAN

From Capernaum, Jesus and his disciples crossed the Sea of Galilee. A storm blew up unexpectedly, but Jesus calmed it. Landing in the region of the Gerasenes, Jesus sent demons out of a man and into a herd of pigs that plunged over the steep bank into the lake.

• **5:11** According to Old Testament law (Leviticus 11:7), pigs were unclean animals. This meant that they could not be eaten or even touched by a Jew. This incident took place southeast of the Sea of Galilee in the region of the Gerasenes, a Gentile region, which explains how a herd of pigs could be involved.

5:15
Matt 4:24

5:18
Ps 116:12

5:20
Ps 116:16
Isa 63:7
1 Tim 1:13-14

¹⁴The herdsmen fled to the nearby town and the surrounding countryside, spreading the news as they ran. People rushed out to see what had happened. ¹⁵A crowd soon gathered around Jesus, and they saw the man who had been possessed by the legion of demons. He was sitting there fully clothed and perfectly sane, and they were all afraid. ¹⁶Then those who had seen what happened told the others about the demon-possessed man and the pigs. ¹⁷And the crowd began pleading with Jesus to go away and leave them alone.

¹⁸As Jesus was getting into the boat, the man who had been demon possessed begged to go with him. ¹⁹But Jesus said, "No, go home to your family, and tell them everything the Lord has done for you and how merciful he has been." ²⁰So the man started off to visit the Ten Towns* of that region and began to proclaim the great things Jesus had done for him; and everyone was amazed at what he told them.

5:20 Greek *Decapolis.*

THE TOUCH OF JESUS

What kind of people did Jesus associate with? Whom did he consider important enough to touch? Here we see many of the people Jesus came to know. Some reached out to him; he reached out to them all. Regardless of how great or unknown, rich or poor, young or old, sinner or saint—Jesus cares equally for all. No person is beyond the loving touch of Jesus.

Jesus talked with . . .	*Reference*
A despised tax collector	Matthew 9:9
An insane hermit	Mark 5:1-15
The Roman governor	Mark 15:1-15
A young boy	Mark 9:17-27
A prominent religious leader	John 3:1-21
A homemaker	Luke 10:38-42
An expert in religious law	Matthew 22:35
A criminal	Luke 23:40-43
A synagogue leader	Mark 5:22
Fishermen	Matthew 4:18-20
A king	Luke 23:7-11
A poor widow	Luke 7:11-17; 21:1-4
A Roman captain	Luke 7:1-10
A group of children	Mark 10:13-16
A prophet	Matthew 3
An adulterous woman	John 8:1-11
The Jewish high council	Luke 22:66-71
A sick woman	Mark 5:25-34
A rich man	Mark 10:17-23
A blind beggar	Mark 10:46
Jewish political leaders	Mark 12:13
A group of women	Luke 8:2, 3
The high priest	Matthew 26:62-68
An outcast with leprosy	Luke 17:11-19
A government official	John 4:46-53
A young girl	Mark 5:41, 42
A traitor	John 13:1-3, 27
A helpless and paralyzed man	Mark 2:1-12
An angry mob of soldiers and guards	John 18:3-9
A woman from a foreign land	Mark 7:25-30
A doubting follower	John 20:24-29
An enemy who hated him	Acts 9:1-9
A Samaritan woman	John 4:1-26

5:17 After such a wonderful miracle of saving a man's life, why did the people want Jesus to leave? They were undoubtedly afraid of his supernatural power. They may have also feared that Jesus would continue destroying their pigs—their livelihood. They would rather give up Jesus than lose their source of income and security.

5:19 Jesus told this man to tell his friends about the miraculous healing. Most of the time, Jesus urged those he healed to keep quiet. Why the difference? (1) The demon-possessed man had been alone and unable to speak. Telling others what Jesus did for him would prove that he was healed. (2) This was mainly a Gentile and pagan area, so Jesus was not expecting great crowds to follow him or religious leaders to hinder him. (3) By sending the man away with this good news, Jesus was expanding his ministry to people who were not Jews.

• **5:19, 20** This man had been demon possessed but became a living example of Jesus' power. He wanted to go with Jesus, but Jesus told him to go home and share his story with his friends. If you have experienced Jesus' power in your life, are you, like this man, enthusiastically sharing the good news with those around you? Just as we would tell others about a doctor who cured a physical disease, we should tell about Christ who cures our sin.

5:20 These Ten Towns were located southeast of the Sea of Galilee. Ten cities, each with its own independent government, formed an alliance for protection and for increased trade opportunities. These cities had been settled several centuries earlier by Greek traders and immigrants. Although Jews also lived in the area, they were not in the majority. Many people from the Ten Towns followed Jesus (Matthew 4:25).

Jesus Heals a Bleeding Woman and Restores a Girl to Life
(89/Matthew 9:18-26; Luke 8:40-56)

²¹Jesus got into the boat again and went back to the other side of the lake, where a large crowd gathered around him on the shore. ²²Then a leader of the local synagogue, whose name was Jairus, arrived. When he saw Jesus, he fell at his feet, ²³pleading fervently with him. "My little daughter is dying," he said. "Please come and lay your hands on her; heal her so she can live."

²⁴Jesus went with him, and all the people followed, crowding around him. ²⁵A woman in the crowd had suffered for twelve years with constant bleeding. ²⁶She had suffered a great deal from many doctors, and over the years she had spent everything she had to pay them, but she had gotten no better. In fact, she had gotten worse. ²⁷She had heard about Jesus, so she came up behind him through the crowd and touched his robe. ²⁸For she thought to herself, "If I can just touch his robe, I will be healed." ²⁹Immediately the bleeding stopped, and she could feel in her body that she had been healed of her terrible condition.

³⁰Jesus realized at once that healing power had gone out from him, so he turned around in the crowd and asked, "Who touched my robe?"

³¹His disciples said to him, "Look at this crowd pressing around you. How can you ask, 'Who touched me?'"

³²But he kept on looking around to see who had done it. ³³Then the frightened woman, trembling at the realization of what had happened to her, came and fell to her knees in front of him and told him what she had done. ³⁴And he said to her, "Daughter, your faith has made you well. Go in peace. Your suffering is over."

³⁵While he was still speaking to her, messengers arrived from the home of Jairus, the leader of the synagogue. They told him, "Your daughter is dead. There's no use troubling the Teacher now."

³⁶But Jesus overheard* them and said to Jairus, "Don't be afraid. Just have faith."

³⁷Then Jesus stopped the crowd and wouldn't let anyone go with him except Peter, James, and John (the brother of James). ³⁸When they came to the home of the synagogue leader, Jesus saw much commotion and weeping and wailing. ³⁹He went inside and asked, "Why all this commotion and weeping? The child isn't dead; she's only asleep."

⁴⁰The crowd laughed at him. But he made them all leave, and he took the girl's father and mother and his three disciples into the room where the girl was lying. ⁴¹Holding her hand, he said to her, *"Talitha koum,"* which means "Little girl, get up!" ⁴²And the girl, who was twelve years old, immediately stood up and walked around! They were overwhelmed and totally amazed. ⁴³Jesus gave them strict orders not to tell anyone what had happened, and then he told them to give her something to eat.

5:36 Or *ignored.*

5:23
Matt 8:3
Mark 6:5; 7:32;
8:23, 25
Luke 4:40; 13:13
Acts 9:12, 17; 28:8
5:25
Lev 15:25-30
5:27
Mark 3:10
Acts 19:11-12
5:30
Luke 6:19
5:34
Mark 10:52
Luke 7:50; 17:19;
18:42
Acts 14:9
5:36
John 11:25-40
5:39
John 11:11
5:40
Acts 9:40
5:41-42
Luke 7:14
5:43
Matt 8:4
Mark 1:44; 7:36

5:22 Jesus went back across the Sea of Galilee, probably landing at Capernaum. Jairus was the elected leader of the local synagogue, responsible for supervising worship, running the weekly school, and caring for the building. Many synagogue leaders had close ties to the Pharisees. It is likely, therefore, that some synagogue rulers had been pressured not to support Jesus. For Jairus to bow before Jesus was a significant and perhaps daring act of respect and worship.

• **5:25-34** This woman had a seemingly incurable condition causing her to bleed constantly. This may have been a menstrual or uterine disorder that would have made her ritually unclean (Leviticus 15:25-27) and excluded her from most social contact. She desperately wanted Jesus to heal her, but she knew that her bleeding would cause Jesus to be unclean under Jewish law if she touched him. Sometimes we feel that our problems will keep us from God. But he is always ready to help, no matter how impossible the problem seems to us. We should never allow our fear to keep us from approaching him.

5:31 It was virtually impossible to get close to Jesus, but one woman fought her way desperately through the crowd in order to touch him. As soon as she did, she was healed. What a difference between the crowds who are curious about Jesus and the few who reach out and touch him! Today, many people are vaguely familiar with Jesus, but nothing in their lives is changed or bettered by this passing acquaintance. It is only faith that releases God's healing power. Move beyond curiosity. Reach out to Christ in faith. That touch will change your life forever.

5:35, 36 Jairus's crisis made him feel confused, afraid, and without hope. Jesus' words to Jairus in the midst of crisis speak to us as well: "Don't be afraid. Just have faith." In Jesus, there is both hope and promise. The next time you feel hopeless and afraid, look at your problem from Jesus' point of view. Then don't be afraid; just have faith.

5:38 Loud weeping and wailing were customary at a person's death. Lack of them was the ultimate disgrace and disrespect. Some people, usually women, made mourning a profession and were paid by the dead person's family to weep over the body. On the day of death, the body was carried through the streets, followed by mourners, family members, and friends.

• **5:39, 40** The mourners laughed at Jesus when he said, "The child isn't dead; she's only asleep." The girl was dead, but Jesus used the image of sleep to indicate that her condition was temporary and that she would be restored.

Jesus tolerated the crowd's abuse in order to teach an important lesson about maintaining hope and trust in him. Today, most of the world laughs at Christ's claims. When you are belittled for expressing faith in Jesus and hope for eternal life, remember that unbelievers don't see from God's perspective. For a clear statement about life after death, see 1 Thessalonians 4:13, 14.

• **5:41, 42** Jesus not only demonstrated great power, he also showed tremendous compassion. Jesus' power over nature, evil spirits, and death was motivated by compassion—for a demon-possessed man who lived among tombs, a diseased woman, and the family of a dead girl. The rabbis of the day

The People of Nazareth Refuse to Believe (**91**/Matthew 13:53-58)

6 Jesus left that part of the country and returned with his disciples to Nazareth, his home-town. 2 The next Sabbath he began teaching in the synagogue, and many who heard him were amazed. They asked, "Where did he get all this wisdom and the power to perform such miracles?" 3 Then they scoffed, "He's just a carpenter, the son of Mary* and the brother of James, Joseph,* Judas, and Simon. And his sisters live right here among us." They were deeply offended and refused to believe in him.

4 Then Jesus told them, "A prophet is honored everywhere except in his own hometown

6:2
John 7:15

6:3
John 6:42

6:4
John 4:44

6:3a Some manuscripts read *He's just the son of the carpenter and of Mary.*   **6:3b** Most manuscripts read *Joses;* see Matt 13:55.

HEROD ANTIPAS

Most people dislike having their sins pointed out, especially in public. The shame of being exposed is often stronger than the guilt brought on by the wrongdoing. Herod Antipas was a man experiencing both guilt and shame.

Herod's ruthless ambition was public knowledge, as was his illegal marriage to his brother's wife, Herodias. One man made Herod's sin a public issue. That man was John the Baptist. John had been preaching in the wilderness, and thousands flocked to hear him. Apparently it was no secret that John had rebuked Herod for his adulterous marriage. Herodias was particularly anxious to have John silenced. As a solution, Herod imprisoned John.

Herod liked John. John was probably one of the few people he met who spoke only the truth to him. But the truth about his sin was a bitter pill to swallow, and Herod wavered at the point of conflict: He couldn't afford to have John constantly reminding the people of their leader's sinfulness, but he was afraid to have John killed. He put off the choice. Eventually Herodias forced his hand, and John was executed. Of course, this only served to increase Herod's guilt.

Upon hearing about Jesus, Herod immediately identified him with John. He couldn't decide what to do about Jesus. He didn't want to repeat the mistake he had made with John, so he tried to threaten Jesus just before Jesus' final journey to Jerusalem. When the two met briefly during Jesus' trial, Jesus would not speak to Herod. Herod had proved himself a poor listener to John, and Jesus had nothing to add to John's words. Herod responded with spite and mocking. Having rejected the messenger, he found it easy to reject the Messiah.

For each person, God chooses the best possible ways to reveal himself. He uses his Word, various circumstances, our minds, or other people to get our attention. He is persuasive and persistent but never forces himself on us. To miss or resist God's message, as did Herod, is a tragedy. How aware are you of God's attempts to enter your life? Have you welcomed him?

Strengths and accomplishments	• Built the city of Tiberias and oversaw other architectural projects • Ruled the region of Galilee for the Romans
Weaknesses and mistakes	• Consumed with his quest for power • Put off decisions or made wrong ones under pressure • Divorced his wife to marry the wife of his half brother, Philip • Imprisoned John the Baptist and later ordered his execution • Had a minor part in the execution of Jesus
Lessons from his life	• A life motivated by ambition is usually characterized by self-destruction • Opportunities to do good usually come to us in the form of choices to be made
Vital statistics	• Where: Jerusalem • Occupation: Roman ruler of the region of Galilee and Perea • Relatives: Father: Herod the Great. Mother: Malthace. First wife: daughter of Aretas IV. Second wife: Herodias. • Contemporaries: John the Baptist, Jesus, Pilate
Key verse	"Herod was greatly disturbed whenever he talked with John, but even so, he liked to listen to him" (Mark 6:20).

Herod Antipas's story is told in the Gospels. He is also mentioned in Acts 4:27; 13:1.

considered such people unclean. Polite society avoided them. But Jesus reached out and helped.

5:43 Jesus told the girl's parents not to spread the news of the miracle. He wanted the facts to speak for themselves, and the time was not yet right for a major confrontation with the religious leaders. Jesus still had much to accomplish, and he didn't want people following him just to see his miracles.

6:4 Jesus said that a prophet (in other words, a worker for God) is never honored in his hometown. But that doesn't make his work any less important. A person doesn't need to be respected or honored to be useful to God. If friends, neighbors, or family don't respect your Christian work, don't let their rejection keep you from serving God.

and among his relatives and his own family." ⁵And because of their unbelief, he couldn't do any miracles among them except to place his hands on a few sick people and heal them. ⁶And he was amazed at their unbelief.

6:5
Matt 9:18

Jesus Sends Out the Twelve Disciples (93/Matthew 10:1-15; Luke 9:1-6)

Then Jesus went from village to village, teaching the people. ⁷And he called his twelve disciples together and began sending them out two by two, giving them authority to cast out evil* spirits. ⁸He told them to take nothing for their journey except a walking stick—no food, no traveler's bag, no money.* ⁹He allowed them to wear sandals but not to take a change of clothes.

6:7
Luke 10:1

6:8-9
Matt 10:9-10
Luke 9:3; 10:4

¹⁰"Wherever you go," he said, "stay in the same house until you leave town. ¹¹But if any place refuses to welcome you or listen to you, shake its dust from your feet as you leave to show that you have abandoned those people to their fate."

6:10
Luke 10:7
6:11
Luke 10:11
Acts 13:51

¹²So the disciples went out, telling everyone they met to repent of their sins and turn to God. ¹³And they cast out many demons and healed many sick people, anointing them with olive oil.

6:13
Luke 10:34
Jas 5:14

Herod Kills John the Baptist (95/Matthew 14:1-12; Luke 9:7-9)

¹⁴Herod Antipas, the king, soon heard about Jesus, because everyone was talking about him. Some were saying,* "This must be John the Baptist raised from the dead. That is why he can do such miracles." ¹⁵Others said, "He's the prophet Elijah." Still others said, "He's a prophet like the other great prophets of the past."

6:15
Matt 16:14

¹⁶When Herod heard about Jesus, he said, "John, the man I beheaded, has come back from the dead."

¹⁷For Herod had sent soldiers to arrest and imprison John as a favor to Herodias. She had been his brother Philip's wife, but Herod had married her. ¹⁸John had been telling Herod,

6:17-18
Lev 18:15-16;
20:21
Luke 3:19-20

6:7 Greek *unclean.*   **6:8** Greek *no copper coins in their money belts.*   **6:14** Some manuscripts read *He was saying.*

6:5 Jesus could have done greater miracles in Nazareth, but he chose not to because of the people's pride and unbelief. The miracles he did had little effect on the people because they did not accept his message or believe that he was from God. Therefore, Jesus looked elsewhere, seeking those who would respond to his miracles and message.

6:7 The disciples were sent out in pairs. Individually they could have reached more areas of the country, but this was not Christ's plan. The advantages in going out by twos include: (1) They could strengthen and encourage each other. (2) They could provide comfort in rejection. (3) They could give each other discernment, and fewer mistakes would be made. (4) They could stir each other to action as a counter to idleness or indifference. Our strength comes from God, but he meets many of

our needs through our teamwork with others. As you serve Christ, don't try to go it alone.

6:8, 9 Mark records that the disciples were instructed to take nothing with them *except* walking sticks, while Matthew and Luke record that Jesus told them *not* to take walking sticks. One explanation is that Matthew and Luke were referring to a club used for protection, whereas Mark was talking about a shepherd's crook. In any case, the point in all three accounts is the same—the disciples were to leave at once, without extensive preparation, trusting in God's care rather than in their own resources.

● **6:11** Pious Jews shook the dust from their feet after passing through Gentile cities or territory to show their separation from Gentile influences and practices. When the disciples shook the dust from their feet after leaving a *Jewish* town, it was a vivid sign that they wished to remain separate from people who had rejected Jesus and his message. Jesus made it clear that all who heard the gospel were responsible for what they did with it. The disciples were not to blame if the message was rejected, as long as they had faithfully and carefully presented it. We are not responsible when others reject Christ's message of salvation, but we do have the responsibility to share the Good News clearly and faithfully.

● **6:14, 15** Herod, along with many others, wondered who Jesus really was. Unable to accept Jesus' claim to be God's Son, many people made up their own explanations for his power and authority. Herod thought that Jesus was John the Baptist come back to life, while those who were familiar with the Old Testament thought he was Elijah (Malachi 4:5). Still others believed that Jesus was a teaching prophet in the tradition of Moses, Isaiah, or Jeremiah. Today people still have to make up their minds about Jesus. Some think that if they can name what he is—prophet, teacher, good man—they can weaken the power of his claim on their lives. But what they *think* does not change who Jesus *is.*

PREACHING IN GALILEE
After returning to his hometown, Nazareth, from Capernaum, Jesus preached in the villages of Galilee and sent his disciples out to preach as well. After meeting back in Capernaum, they left by boat to rest, only to be met by the crowds who followed the boat along the shore.

● **6:17-19** Palestine was divided into four territories, each with a different ruler. Herod Antipas, called Herod in the Gospels, was ruler over Galilee; his brother Philip ruled over Traconitis and Iturea. Philip's wife was Herodias, but she had left him to marry

"It is against God's law for you to marry your brother's wife." ¹⁹So Herodias bore a grudge against John and wanted to kill him. But without Herod's approval she was powerless, ²⁰for Herod respected John; and knowing that he was a good and holy man, he protected him. Herod was greatly disturbed whenever he talked with John, but even so, he liked to listen to him.

²¹Herodias's chance finally came on Herod's birthday. He gave a party for his high government officials, army officers, and the leading citizens of Galilee. ²²Then his daughter, also named Herodias,* came in and performed a dance that greatly pleased Herod and his guests. "Ask me for anything you like," the king said to the girl, "and I will give it to you." ²³He even vowed, "I will give you whatever you ask, up to half my kingdom!"

6:23
Esth 5:3-6; 7:2

²⁴She went out and asked her mother, "What should I ask for?"

Her mother told her, "Ask for the head of John the Baptist!"

²⁵So the girl hurried back to the king and told him, "I want the head of John the Baptist, right now, on a tray!"

²⁶Then the king deeply regretted what he had said; but because of the vows he had made in front of his guests, he couldn't refuse her. ²⁷So he immediately sent an executioner to the prison to cut off John's head and bring it to him. The soldier beheaded John in the prison, ²⁸brought his head on a tray, and gave it to the girl, who took it to her mother. ²⁹When John's disciples heard what had happened, they came to get his body and buried it in a tomb.

Jesus Feeds Five Thousand (**96**/Matthew 14:13-21; Luke 9:10-17; John 6:1-15)

6:30
Luke 9:10; 10:17
6:31
Mark 3:20

³⁰The apostles returned to Jesus from their ministry tour and told him all they had done and taught. ³¹Then Jesus said, "Let's go off by ourselves to a quiet place and rest awhile." He said this because there were so many people coming and going that Jesus and his apostles didn't even have time to eat.

6:34
†Num 27:17
†1 Kgs 22:17
†2 Chr 18:16
†Zech 10:2
Matt 9:36

³²So they left by boat for a quiet place, where they could be alone. ³³But many people recognized them and saw them leaving, and people from many towns ran ahead along the shore and got there ahead of them. ³⁴Jesus saw the huge crowd as he stepped from the boat, and he had compassion on them because they were like sheep without a shepherd. So he began teaching them many things.

6:22 Some manuscripts read *the daughter of Herodias herself.*

REAL LEADERSHIP Mark gives us some of the best insights into Jesus' character.	Herod as a leader	Jesus as a leader
	Selfish	Compassionate
	Murderer	Healer
	Immoral	Just and good
	Political opportunist	Servant
	King over small territory	King over all creation

---

Herod Antipas. When John confronted the two for committing adultery, Herodias formulated a plot to kill him. Instead of trying to get rid of her sin, Herodias tried to get rid of the one who brought it to public attention. This is also exactly what the religious leaders were trying to do to Jesus.

6:18 Christians today face a world of moral compromise. Secular power sets standards that correspond to majority vote; Christian standards, however, begin and end with God's Word. To be faithful to God's Word, we must stand up against what is morally wrong. Responsible Christians must choose their battles. Start with prayers for wisdom, then prayers for courage. Once your battle is chosen, speak and act as a faithful follower of the living God. Witness with strength; move mountains by faith; overcome in love. Show the compromised world a little of John's stubbornness, fortitude, and faith.

• **6:20** Herod arrested John the Baptist under pressure from his wife and advisers. Though Herod respected John's integrity, in the end Herod had John killed because of pressure from his peers and family. What you do under pressure often shows what you are really like.

• **6:22, 23** As a ruler under Roman authority, Herod had no kingdom to give. The offer of half his kingdom was Herod's way to say

that he would give Herodias's daughter almost anything she wanted. When Herodias asked for John's head, Herod would have been greatly embarrassed in front of his guests if he had denied her request. Words are powerful. Because they can lead to great sin, we should use them with great care.

6:30 Mark uses the word *apostles* here and in 3:14. *Apostle* means "one sent" as messenger, authorized agent, or missionary. The word became an official title for Jesus' 12 disciples after his death and resurrection (Acts 1:25, 26; Ephesians 2:20).

6:31 When the disciples had returned from their mission, Jesus took them away to rest. Doing God's work is very important, but Jesus recognized that to do it effectively we need periodic rest and renewal. Jesus and his disciples, however, did not always find it easy to get the rest they needed!

6:34 This crowd was as pitiful as a flock of sheep without a shepherd. Sheep are easily scattered; without a shepherd they are in grave danger. Jesus was the Shepherd who could teach them what they needed to know and keep them from straying from God. See Psalm 23; Isaiah 40:11; Ezekiel 34:5ff; and John 10:11-16 for descriptions of the good shepherd.

35Late in the afternoon his disciples came to him and said, "This is a remote place, and it's already getting late. 36Send the crowds away so they can go to the nearby farms and villages and buy something to eat."

37But Jesus said, "You feed them."

"With what?" they asked. "We'd have to work for months to earn enough money* to buy food for all these people!"

38"How much bread do you have?" he asked. "Go and find out."

They came back and reported, "We have five loaves of bread and two fish."

39Then Jesus told the disciples to have the people sit down in groups on the green grass. 40So they sat down in groups of fifty or a hundred.

41Jesus took the five loaves and two fish, looked up toward heaven, and blessed them. Then, breaking the loaves into pieces, he kept giving the bread to the disciples so they could distribute it to the people. He also divided the fish for everyone to share. 42They all ate as much as they wanted, 43and afterward, the disciples picked up twelve baskets of leftover bread and fish. 44A total of 5,000 men and their families were fed from those loaves!

6:37
2 Kgs 4:42-44
Matt 15:33
Mark 8:4

6:38
Matt 15:34
Mark 8:5

6:41
Matt 14:19

Jesus Walks on Water (**97**/Matthew 14:22-23; John 6:16-21)

45Immediately after this, Jesus insisted that his disciples get back into the boat and head across the lake to Bethsaida, while he sent the people home. 46After telling everyone good-bye, he went up into the hills by himself to pray.

47Late that night, the disciples were in their boat in the middle of the lake, and Jesus was alone on land. 48He saw that they were in serious trouble, rowing hard and struggling against the wind and waves. About three o'clock in the morning* Jesus came toward them, walking on the water. He intended to go past them, 49but when they saw him walking on the water, they cried out in terror, thinking he was a ghost. 50They were all terrified when they saw him.

But Jesus spoke to them at once. "Don't be afraid," he said. "Take courage! I am here!*"

51Then he climbed into the boat, and the wind stopped. They were totally amazed, 52for they still didn't understand the significance of the miracle of the loaves. Their hearts were too hard to take it in.

6:52
Mark 8:17-21

6:37 Greek *It would take 200 denarii.* A denarius was equivalent to a laborer's full day's wage.　**6:48** Greek *About the fourth watch of the night.*　**6:50** Or *The 'I AM' is here;* Greek reads *I am.* See Exod 3:14.

6:37-42 When Jesus asked the disciples to provide food for over 5,000 people, they were amazed and said it would take a small fortune to feed such a crowd. How do you react when you are given an impossible task? A situation that seems impossible with human resources is simply an opportunity for God. The disciples did everything they could by gathering the available food and organizing the people into groups. Then, in answer to prayer, God did the impossible. When facing a seemingly impossible task, do what you can and ask God to do the rest. He may see fit to make the impossible happen.

6:37-42 Why did Jesus bother to feed these people? He could just as easily have sent them on their way. Jesus does not ignore needs, however. He is concerned with every aspect of our lives—the physical as well as the spiritual.

We might well ask why the church has taken so lightly the command, "You feed them." Jesus' compassion for these hungry people is recorded in all four Gospels. For people who are desperately hungry, there is no better way for us to show God's love to them than to help to provide for their physical needs. As we work to bring wholeness to people's lives, we must never ignore the fact that all of us have both physical and spiritual needs. It is impossible to minister effectively to the spiritual need without considering the physical need. (See also James 2:14-17.)

6:49, 50 The disciples were afraid, but Jesus' presence calmed their fears. When you experience fear, do you try to deal with it yourself, or do you let Jesus deal with it? In times of fear and uncertainty, it is calming to know that Christ is always with you (Matthew 28:20). To recognize Christ's presence is the antidote for fear.

6:52 The disciples didn't want to believe, perhaps because (1) they couldn't accept the fact that this human named Jesus was really the Son of God; (2) they dared not believe that the Messiah would choose them as his followers; (3) they still did not understand the real purpose for Jesus' coming to earth. Their disbelief took the form of misunderstanding. Even after watching Jesus miraculously feed 5,000 people, they still could not take the final step of faith and believe that he was God's Son. If they had, they would not have been amazed that Jesus could walk on water.

JESUS WALKS ON THE WATER
After feeding the people who had followed to hear him at Bethsaida, Jesus sent the people home, sent his disciples by boat toward Bethsaida, and went to pray. The disciples encountered a storm, and Jesus walked to them on the water. They landed at Gennesaret.

Jesus Heals All Who Touch Him (**98**/Matthew 14:34-36)

⁵³After they had crossed the lake, they landed at Gennesaret. They brought the boat to shore ⁵⁴and climbed out. The people recognized Jesus at once, ⁵⁵and they ran throughout the whole area, carrying sick people on mats to wherever they heard he was. ⁵⁶Wherever he went—in villages, cities, or the countryside—they brought the sick out to the marketplaces. They begged him to let the sick touch at least the fringe of his robe, and all who touched him were healed.

6:56
Matt 9:20
Mark 5:27
Luke 8:44

Jesus Teaches about Inner Purity (**102**/Matthew 15:1-20)

7 One day some Pharisees and teachers of religious law arrived from Jerusalem to see Jesus. ²They noticed that some of his disciples failed to follow the Jewish ritual of hand washing before eating. ³(The Jews, especially the Pharisees, do not eat until they have poured water over their cupped hands,* as required by their ancient traditions. ⁴Similarly, they don't eat anything from the market until they immerse their hands* in water. This is but one of many traditions they have clung to—such as their ceremonial washing of cups, pitchers, and kettles.*)

7:2
Luke 11:38
Acts 10:14, 28
7:3
Gal 1:14
Col 2:8
7:4
Matt 23:25
Luke 11:39

⁵So the Pharisees and teachers of religious law asked him, "Why don't your disciples follow our age-old tradition? They eat without first performing the hand-washing ceremony."

⁶Jesus replied, "You hypocrites! Isaiah was right when he prophesied about you, for he wrote,

7:6-7
†Isa 29:13
Col 2:22

'These people honor me with their lips,
  but their hearts are far from me.
⁷ Their worship is a farce,
  for they teach man-made ideas as commands from God.'*

7:3 Greek *have washed with the fist.*   **7:4a** Some manuscripts read *sprinkle themselves.*   **7:4b** Some manuscripts add *and dining couches.*   **7:7** Isa 29:13 (Greek version).

GOSPEL ACCOUNTS FOUND ONLY IN MARK	Section	Topic	Significance
	4:26-29	Story of the growing seed	We must share the Good News of Jesus with other people, but only God makes it grow in their lives.
	7:31-37	Jesus heals a deaf man who could hardly talk	Jesus cares about our physical as well as spiritual needs.
	8:22-26	Jesus heals the blind man at Bethsaida	Jesus is considerate because he makes sure this man's sight is fully restored.

Is your heart hardened against Jesus? Even Christians can be hard-hearted to Jesus' word. We can be informed about what his Word says, and we can be amazed at how he has worked in other people's lives, but we can refuse to believe he will come to our aid in our time of trouble. Such a reaction is not unbelief, but willful, hard-hearted rejection of Christ's ability to help. Instead, "take courage," and trust that he is there for you.

6:53 Gennesaret was a small fertile plain located on the west side of the Sea of Galilee. Capernaum, Jesus' home, sat at the northern edge of this plain.

• **7:1ff** The religious leaders sent some investigators from their headquarters in Jerusalem to check up on Jesus. The delegation didn't like what they found, however, because Jesus scolded them for keeping the law and the traditions in order to look holy instead of to honor God. The prophet Isaiah accused the religious leaders of his day of doing the same thing (Isaiah 29:13). Jesus used Isaiah's words to accuse these men.

• **7:3, 4** Mark explained these Jewish rituals because he was writing to a non-Jewish audience. Before each meal, devout Jews performed a short ceremony, washing their hands and arms in a specific way. The disciples did not have dirty hands, but they were simply not carrying out this traditional cleansing. The Pharisees thought this ceremony cleansed them from any contact they might have had with anything considered unclean. Jesus said they were wrong in thinking they were acceptable to God just because they were clean on the outside.

7:4 Christians become like Pharisees when they worry that contact with unbelievers may leave them tainted—avoiding "worldly" places where sinners hang out or rejecting books or speakers whose ideas do not conform to theirs. Some Christians and some Pharisees have a lot in common: Both would try to stop Jesus from working certain places or talking to certain people. Jesus wants us to go out into the world and make contact. Jesus didn't intend for us to withdraw, purify ourselves, and never reach out.

• **7:6, 7** Hypocrisy is pretending to be something you are not and have no intention of being. Jesus called the Pharisees hypocrites because they worshiped God for the wrong reasons. Their worship was not motivated by love but by a desire to attain profit, to appear holy, and to increase their status. We become hypocrites when we (1) pay more attention to reputation than to character, (2) carefully follow certain religious practices while allowing our hearts to remain distant from God, and (3) emphasize our virtues but others' sins.

8 For you ignore God's law and substitute your own tradition."

9 Then he said, "You skillfully sidestep God's law in order to hold on to your own tradition. 10 For instance, Moses gave you this law from God: 'Honor your father and mother,'* and 'Anyone who speaks disrespectfully of father or mother must be put to death.'* 11 But you say it is all right for people to say to their parents, 'Sorry, I can't help you. For I have vowed to give to God what I would have given to you.'* 12 In this way, you let them disregard their needy parents. 13 And so you cancel the word of God in order to hand down your own tradition. And this is only one example among many others."

14 Then Jesus called to the crowd to come and hear. "All of you listen," he said, "and try to understand. 15 It's not what goes into your body that defiles you; you are defiled by what comes from your heart.*"

17 Then Jesus went into a house to get away from the crowd, and his disciples asked him what he meant by the parable he had just used. 18 "Don't you understand either?" he asked. "Can't you see that the food you put into your body cannot defile you? 19 Food doesn't go into your heart, but only passes through the stomach and then goes into the sewer." (By saying this, he declared that every kind of food is acceptable in God's eyes.)

20 And then he added, "It is what comes from inside that defiles you. 21 For from within, out of a person's heart, come evil thoughts, sexual immorality, theft, murder, 22 adultery, greed, wickedness, deceit, lustful desires, envy, slander, pride, and foolishness. 23 All these vile things come from within; they are what defile you."

7:9
Isa 24:4-5
7:10
†Exod 20:12; 21:17
†Lev 20:9
†Deut 5:16
1 Tim 5:8

7:15
1 Cor 8:8
1 Tim 4:4

7:17
Mark 9:28

7:19
Acts 10:15; 11:9
Rom 14:1-12
Col 2:16
1 Tim 4:3-5

7:21-22
Rom 1:29-31
Gal 5:19-21
Titus 1:15

2. Jesus' ministry beyond Galilee

Jesus Sends a Demon Out of a Girl (**103**/Matthew 15:21-28)

24 Then Jesus left Galilee and went north to the region of Tyre.* He didn't want anyone to know which house he was staying in, but he couldn't keep it a secret. 25 Right away a woman

7:10a Exod 20:12; Deut 5:16.   **7:10b** Exod 21:17 (Greek version); Lev 20:9 (Greek version).   **7:11** Greek *'What I would have given to you is Corban' (that is, a gift).*   **7:15** Some manuscripts add verse 16, *Anyone with ears to hear should listen and understand.* Compare 4:9, 23.   **7:24** Some manuscripts add *and Sidon.*

• **7:8, 9** The Pharisees had added hundreds of their own rules and regulations to God's holy laws, and then they tried to force people to follow these rules. These men claimed to know God's will in every detail of life. There are still religious leaders today who add rules and regulations to God's Word, causing much confusion among believers. It is idolatry to claim that your interpretation of God's Word is as important as God's Word itself. It is especially dangerous to set up unbiblical standards for *others* to follow. Instead, look to Christ for guidance about your own behavior, and let him lead others in the details of their lives.

7:8, 9 Jesus wasn't against all tradition, but he was against those who made their traditions as important, if not more important, than God's Word. Good traditions shine a spotlight on God's Word, move us to obedient service, and help our hearts sing. They explain

and reinforce the teachings of God. God's Word should always be the focus, and tradition a means of bringing that Word alive. Celebrate your traditions with the prayer that Christ would be exalted. Change your traditions if they become more important than God's Word.

• **7:10, 11** The Pharisees used God as an excuse to avoid helping their families. They thought it was more important to put money in the Temple treasury than to help their needy parents, although God's law specifically says to honor fathers and mothers (Exodus 20:12) and to care for those in need (Leviticus 25:35-43). (For vowing to give money to God, see the note on Matthew 15:5, 6.) We should give money and time to God, but we must never use God as an excuse to neglect our responsibilities. Helping those in need is one of the most important ways to honor God.

• **7:18, 19** As they interpreted the dietary laws (Leviticus 11), the Jews believed they could be clean before God because of what they refused to eat. Jesus pointed out that sin begins in the attitudes and intentions of the inner person. Jesus did not degrade the law, but he paved the way for the change made clear in Acts 10:9-29 when God removed the cultural restrictions regarding food. While being concerned about what we put into our bodies is a good, healthy practice, very few people are as stringent about what they put into their minds through reading or watching television. Jesus was more concerned about mind-set and thought processes than about food laws. Do you worry about what foods you eat, but put "junk food" in your mind?

7:20-23 An evil action begins with a single thought. Allowing our mind to dwell on lust, envy, hatred, or revenge will lead to sin. Don't defile yourself by focusing on evil. Instead, follow Paul's advice in Philippians 4:8 and think about what is true, honorable, right, pure, lovely, and admirable.

7:24 Jesus traveled about 30 miles to Tyre. The cities of Tyre and Sidon were port cities on the Mediterranean Sea north of Israel. Both had flourishing trade and were very wealthy. They were proud, historic Canaanite cities.

In David's day, Tyre was on friendly terms with Israel (2 Samuel 5:11), but soon afterward the city became known for its wicked-

MINISTRY IN PHOENICIA
Jesus' ministry was to all people— first to Jews but also to Gentiles. Jesus took his disciples from Galilee to Tyre and Sidon, large cities in Phoenicia, where he healed a Gentile woman's daughter.

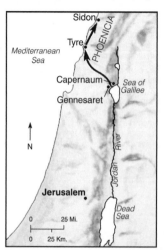

who had heard about him came and fell at his feet. Her little girl was possessed by an evil* spirit, 26 and she begged him to cast out the demon from her daughter.

Since she was a Gentile, born in Syrian Phoenicia, 27 Jesus told her, "First I should feed the children—my own family, the Jews.* It isn't right to take food from the children and throw it to the dogs."

28 She replied, "That's true, Lord, but even the dogs under the table are allowed to eat the scraps from the children's plates."

29 "Good answer!" he said. "Now go home, for the demon has left your daughter." 30 And when she arrived home, she found her little girl lying quietly in bed, and the demon was gone.

Jesus Heals Many People (**104**/Matthew 15:29-31)

31 Jesus left Tyre and went up to Sidon before going back to the Sea of Galilee and the region of the Ten Towns.* 32 A deaf man with a speech impediment was brought to him, and the people begged Jesus to lay his hands on the man to heal him.

33 Jesus led him away from the crowd so they could be alone. He put his fingers into the man's ears. Then, spitting on his own fingers, he touched the man's tongue. 34 Looking up to heaven, he sighed and said, *"Ephphatha,"* which means, "Be opened!" 35 Instantly the man could hear perfectly, and his tongue was freed so he could speak plainly!

36 Jesus told the crowd not to tell anyone, but the more he told them not to, the more they spread the news. 37 They were completely amazed and said again and again, "Everything he does is wonderful. He even makes the deaf to hear and gives speech to those who cannot speak."

Jesus Feeds Four Thousand (**105**/Matthew 15:32-39)

8 About this time another large crowd had gathered, and the people ran out of food again. Jesus called his disciples and told them, 2 "I feel sorry for these people. They have been here with me for three days, and they have nothing left to eat. 3 If I send them home hungry, they will faint along the way. For some of them have come a long distance."

4 His disciples replied, "How are we supposed to find enough food to feed them out here in the wilderness?"

5 Jesus asked, "How much bread do you have?"

"Seven loaves," they replied.

7:33
Mark 8:23
John 9:6

7:34
Matt 14:19
Mark 6:41
John 11:41; 17:1

7:36
Matt 8:4

7:37
Isa 35:5-6

8:1-10
Mark 6:32-44

8:2
Matt 9:36

8:4
Num 11:21-22
2 Kgs 4:42-43

7:25 Greek *unclean.*   **7:27** Greek *Let the children eat first.*   **7:31** Greek *Decapolis.*

---

ness. Its king even claimed to be God (Ezekiel 28:1ff). Tyre rejoiced when Jerusalem was destroyed in 586 B.C., because without Israel's competition, Tyre's trade and profits would increase. It was into this evil and materialistic culture that Jesus brought his message.

7:26 This woman is called a Gentile, born in Syrian Phoenicia. Mark's designation refers to her political background. His Roman audience would easily identify her by the part of the empire that was her home.

7:27, 28 On the surface, Jesus' words may seem harsh and unsympathetic, but the woman recognized them as a wide-open door to God's throne. Jesus did not use the negative term for "dogs" that referred to scavengers (the word sometimes used by Jews to refer to Gentiles); instead, he used the term for a household pet. The woman took the cue and added to his analogy of pets under a family dining table. Her attitude was expectant and hopeful, not prickly or hypersensitive. She knew what she wanted and she believed Jesus could provide. We could learn from this woman's singular purpose and optimistic resilience. Jesus really does want to meet our needs. When we pray, we're talking to a friend.

7:29 This miracle shows that Jesus' power over demons is so great that he doesn't need to be present physically in order to free someone. His power transcends any distance.

7:34 When Jesus said, "Be opened!" he used language that this deaf man would understand. The healing message was personal and unique. Whoever thought spittle might be the conduit of a miracle? If there is only one means of witness in your church (sermons, for instance), many people likely will not hear. Churches need lots of different methods to meet diverse needs. Let musi-

cians play, singers sing, actors act, and writers write. Let each creative Christian tell the story. Jesus used spit and mud; surely we can find windows to the minds and hearts of people as well.

8:1ff This is a different miracle from the feeding of the 5,000 described in chapter 6. At that time, those fed were mostly Jews. This time Jesus was ministering to a non-Jewish crowd in the Gentile region of the Ten Towns. Jesus' actions and message were beginning to have an impact on large numbers of Gentiles. That Jesus would compassionately minister to non-Jews was very reassuring to Mark's primarily Roman audience.

8:1-3 Do you ever feel that God is so busy with important concerns that he can't possibly be aware of your needs? Just as Jesus was concerned about these people's need for food, he is concerned about our daily needs. At another time Jesus said, "Your heavenly Father already knows all your needs" (Matthew 6:32). Do you have concerns that you think would not interest God? Nothing is too large for him to handle and no need too small to escape his interest.

8:4 How could the disciples experience so many of Jesus' miracles and yet be so slow to comprehend who he was? They had already seen Jesus feed over 5,000 people with five loaves and two fish (6:35-44), yet here they doubted whether he could feed another large group.

Sometimes we are also slow to catch on. Although Christ has brought us through trials and temptations in the past, we don't believe that he will do so in the future. Is your heart too closed to take in all that God can do for you? Don't be like the disciples. Remember what Christ has done, and have faith that he will do it again.

6So Jesus told all the people to sit down on the ground. Then he took the seven loaves, thanked God for them, and broke them into pieces. He gave them to his disciples, who distributed the bread to the crowd. 7A few small fish were found, too, so Jesus also blessed these and told the disciples to distribute them.

8:7
Matt 14:19

8They ate as much as they wanted. Afterward, the disciples picked up seven large baskets of leftover food. 9There were about 4,000 people in the crowd that day, and Jesus sent them home after they had eaten. 10Immediately after this, he got into a boat with his disciples and crossed over to the region of Dalmanutha.

8:10
Matt 15:39

Leaders Demand a Miraculous Sign (**106**/Matthew 16:1-4)

11When the Pharisees heard that Jesus had arrived, they came and started to argue with him. Testing him, they demanded that he show them a miraculous sign from heaven to prove his authority.

8:11-21
Luke 11:16, 29
John 6:30

12When he heard this, he sighed deeply in his spirit and said, "Why do these people keep demanding a miraculous sign? I tell you the truth, I will not give this generation any such sign." 13So he got back into the boat and left them, and he crossed to the other side of the lake.

Jesus Warns against Wrong Teaching (**107**/Matthew 16:5-12)

14But the disciples had forgotten to bring any food. They had only one loaf of bread with them in the boat. 15As they were crossing the lake, Jesus warned them, "Watch out! Beware of the yeast of the Pharisees and of Herod."

8:15
Luke 12:1

16At this they began to argue with each other because they hadn't brought any bread. 17Jesus knew what they were saying, so he said, "Why are you arguing about having no bread? Don't you know or understand even yet? Are your hearts too hard to take it in? 18'You have eyes—can't you see? You have ears—can't you hear?'* Don't you remember anything at all? 19When I fed the 5,000 with five loaves of bread, how many baskets of leftovers did you pick up afterward?"

8:17
Isa 6:9-10
Mark 6:52

8:18
†Jer 5:21
Ezek 12:2
Matt 13:13

"Twelve," they said.

8:19
Mark 6:41-44
Luke 9:17
John 6:13

20"And when I fed the 4,000 with seven loaves, how many large baskets of leftovers did you pick up?"

"Seven," they said.

8:20
Matt 15:37

21"Don't you understand yet?" he asked them.

Jesus Restores Sight to a Blind Man (**108**)

22When they arrived at Bethsaida, some people brought a blind man to Jesus, and they begged him to touch the man and heal him. 23Jesus took the blind man by the hand and led him out of the village. Then, spitting on the man's eyes, he laid his hands on him and asked, "Can you see anything now?"

8:23
Mark 7:33
John 9:6

24The man looked around. "Yes," he said, "I see people, but I can't see them very clearly. They look like trees walking around."

8:18 Jer 5:21.

8:6 Jesus gave thanks for the food, and he serves as a model for us. Life is a gift, and the nourishment life requires, while it comes from the work of many hands, conveys God's material blessing. Mealtime provides an opportunity to thank God for daily needs met, for taste and beauty, and for human company and divine companionship. Giving thanks keeps us from regarding a plate of food as a trough, our stomachs as bottomless pits, and our gathering to eat as a bothersome interruption. Keep up the good tradition of praying and thanking God before your meals. Let your gratefulness to God be genuine.

• **8:11** The Pharisees had tried to explain away Jesus' previous miracles by claiming they were done by luck, coincidence, or evil power. Here they demanded a sign from heaven—something only God could do. Jesus refused their demand because he knew that even this kind of miracle would not convince them. They had already decided not to believe. Hearts can become so hard that even the most convincing facts and demonstrations will not change them.

8:15 Mark mentions the yeast of the Pharisees and of Herod, while Matthew talks about the yeast of the Pharisees and Sad-

ducees. Mark's audience, mostly non-Jews, would have known about Herod but not necessarily about the Jewish religious sect of the Sadducees. Thus, Mark quoted the part of Jesus' statement that his readers would understand. This reference to Herod may mean the supporters of Herod, a group of Jews who supported the king. Many supporters of Herod were also Sadducees. Yeast in this passage symbolizes evil. Just as only a small amount of yeast is needed to make a batch of bread rise, so the hard-heartedness of the religious and political leaders could permeate and contaminate the entire society and make it rise up against Jesus.

8:17, 18 Jesus rebuked the disciples for their hard hearts. Today the Hardhearts believe: (1) that poverty is always caused by laziness; helping the poor only enables them; (2) that worship is best conducted in one way—our way—which has worked very well for forty years, thank you, and need not be changed; (3) that evangelism doesn't apply; people will never change anyway, so we don't need to do it. Joining the Hardhearts requires only one pledge: You must refuse to listen to Jesus' questions. Don't be a Hardheart. Be open to Christ's truth. Let him soften your heart.

²⁵Then Jesus placed his hands on the man's eyes again, and his eyes were opened. His

8:26
Matt 8:4

sight was completely restored, and he could see everything clearly. ²⁶Jesus sent him away, saying, "Don't go back into the village on your way home."

Peter Says Jesus Is the Messiah (109/Matthew 16:13-20; Luke 9:18-20)

8:27-30
John 6:67-71

²⁷Jesus and his disciples left Galilee and went up to the villages near Caesarea Philippi. As they were walking along, he asked them, "Who do people say I am?"

8:28
Matt 14:2

²⁸"Well," they replied, "some say John the Baptist, some say Elijah, and others say you are one of the other prophets."

8:29
Matt 16:20
Luke 9:20
John 6:69; 11:27

²⁹Then he asked them, "But who do you say I am?"

Peter replied, "You are the Messiah.*"

³⁰But Jesus warned them not to tell anyone about him.

Jesus Predicts His Death the First Time (110/Matthew 16:21-28; Luke 9:21-27)

³¹Then Jesus began to tell them that the Son of Man* must suffer many terrible things and be rejected by the elders, the leading priests, and the teachers of religious law. He would be killed, but three days later he would rise from the dead. ³²As he talked about this openly with his disciples, Peter took him aside and began to reprimand him for saying such things.*

³³Jesus turned around and looked at his disciples, then reprimanded Peter. "Get away from me, Satan!" he said. "You are seeing things merely from a human point of view, not from God's."

8:29 Or *the Christ. Messiah* (a Hebrew term) and *Christ* (a Greek term) both mean "the anointed one."   **8:31** "Son of Man" is a title Jesus used for himself.   **8:32** Or *began to correct him.*

8:25 Why did Jesus touch the man a second time before he could see? This miracle was not too difficult for Jesus, but he chose to do it in stages, possibly to show the disciples that some healing would be gradual rather than instantaneous or to demonstrate that spiritual truth is not always perceived clearly at first. Before Jesus left, however, the man was healed completely.

8:27 Caesarea Philippi was an especially pagan city known for its worship of Greek gods and its temples devoted to the ancient god Pan. The ruler Philip, referred to in 6:17, changed the city's name from Caesarea to Caesarea Philippi so that it would not be confused with the coastal city of Caesarea (Acts 8:40), the capital of the territory ruled by his brother Herod Antipas. This pagan city where many gods were recognized was a fitting place for Jesus to ask the disciples to recognize him as the Son of God.

8:28 For the story of John the Baptist, see Mark 1:1-11 and 6:14-29. For the story of Elijah, see 1 Kings 17–20 and 2 Kings 1–2.

8:29 Jesus asked the disciples who other people thought he was; then he asked them the same question. It is not enough to know what others say about Jesus: You must know, understand, and accept for yourself that he is the Messiah. You must move from curiosity to commitment, from admiration to adoration.

8:30 Why did Jesus warn his own disciples not to tell anyone the truth about him? Jesus knew they needed more instruction about the work he would accomplish through his death and resurrection. Without more teaching, the disciples would have only half the picture. When they confessed Jesus as the Christ, they still didn't know all that it meant.

8:31 The name for Jesus, *Son of Man,* is Jesus' most common title for himself. It comes from Daniel 7:13, where the Son of Man is a heavenly figure who, in the end times, has authority and power. The name refers to Jesus as the Messiah, the representative man, the human agent of God who is vindicated by God. In this passage, *Son of Man* is linked closely with Peter's confession of Jesus as the Christ and confirms its messianic significance.

From this point on, Jesus spoke plainly and directly to his disciples about his death and resurrection. He began to prepare them for what was going to happen to him by telling them three times that he would soon die (8:31; 9:31; 10:33, 34).

8:32, 33 In this moment, Peter was not considering God's purposes but only his own natural human desires and feelings. Peter wanted Christ to be king, but not the suffering servant

prophesied in Isaiah 53. He was ready to receive the glory of following the Messiah but not the persecution.

The Christian life is not a paved road to wealth and ease. It often involves hard work, persecution, deprivation, and deep suffering. Peter saw only part of the picture. Don't repeat his mistake. Instead, focus on the good that God can bring out of apparent evil and the Resurrection that follows the Crucifixion.

8:33 Peter was often the spokesman for all the disciples. In singling him out, Jesus may have been addressing all of them indirectly. Unknowingly, the disciples were trying to prevent Jesus from going to the cross and thus fulfilling his mission on earth. Satan also tempted Jesus to avoid the way of the cross (Matthew 4). Whereas Satan's motives were evil, the disciples were motivated by love and admiration for Jesus. Nevertheless, the disciples' job was not to guide and protect Jesus but to follow him. Only after Jesus' death and resurrection would they fully understand why he had to die.

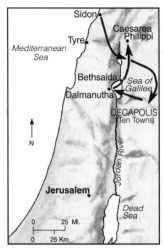

CONTINUED MINISTRY
After taking a roundabout way back to Galilee through Decapolis (the Ten Towns), Jesus returned to Dalmanutha where Jewish leaders questioned his authority. From there he went to Bethsaida and on to Caesarea Philippi. Here he talked with his disciples about his authority and coming events.

34Then, calling the crowd to join his disciples, he said, "If any of you wants to be my fol-lower, you must turn from your selfish ways, take up your cross, and follow me. 35If you try to hang on to your life, you will lose it. But if you give up your life for my sake and for the sake of the Good News, you will save it. 36And what do you benefit if you gain the whole world but lose your own soul?* 37Is anything worth more than your soul? 38If anyone is ashamed of me and my message in these adulterous and sinful days, the Son of Man will be ashamed of that person when he returns in the glory of his Father with the holy angels."

8:34
Matt 10:38
Luke 14:27

8:35
Matt 10:39
Luke 17:33
John 12:25

8:38
Matt 10:33
Luke 12:9

9 Jesus went on to say, "I tell you the truth, some standing here right now will not die before they see the Kingdom of God arrive in great power!"

Jesus is Transfigured on the Mountain (111/Matthew 17:1-13; Luke 9:28-36)

2Six days later Jesus took Peter, James, and John, and led them up a high mountain to be alone. As the men watched, Jesus' appearance was transformed, 3and his clothes became dazzling white, far whiter than any earthly bleach could ever make them. 4Then Elijah and Moses appeared and began talking with Jesus.

9:2-10
2 Pet 1:17-18

9:3
Dan 7:9
Matt 28:3

5Peter exclaimed, "Rabbi, it's wonderful for us to be here! Let's make three shelters as memorials*—one for you, one for Moses, and one for Elijah." 6He said this because he didn't really know what else to say, for they were all terrified.

7Then a cloud overshadowed them, and a voice from the cloud said, "This is my dearly loved Son. Listen to him." 8Suddenly, when they looked around, Moses and Elijah were gone, and they saw only Jesus with them.

9:7
Exod 40:34
Deut 18:15
Heb 1:2; 2:3; 12:25

9As they went back down the mountain, he told them not to tell anyone what they had seen until the Son of Man* had risen from the dead. 10So they kept it to themselves, but they often asked each other what he meant by "rising from the dead."

8:36 Or your self? also in 8:37.   **9:5** Greek three tabernacles.   **9:9** "Son of Man" is a title Jesus used for himself.

• **8:34** The Romans, Mark's original audience, knew what taking up the cross meant. Death on a cross was a form of execution used by Rome for dangerous criminals. A prisoner carried his own cross to the place of execution, signifying submission to Rome's power.

Jesus used the image of carrying a cross to illustrate the ultimate submission required of his followers. He is not against pleasure, nor was he saying that we should seek pain needlessly. Jesus was talking about the heroic effort needed to follow him moment by moment, to do his will even when the work is difficult and the future looks bleak.

8:35 We should be willing to lose our life for the sake of the Good News, not because our life is useless but because nothing—not even life itself—can compare to what we gain with Christ. Jesus wants us to choose to follow him rather than to lead a life of sin and self-satisfaction. He wants us to stop trying to control our own destiny and to let him direct us. This makes good sense because, as the Creator, Christ knows better than we do what real life is about. He asks for submission, not self-hatred; he asks us only to lose our self-centered determination to be in charge.

8:36, 37 Many people spend all their energy seeking pleasure. Jesus said, however, that worldliness, which is centered on possessions, position, or power, is ultimately worthless. Whatever you have on earth is only temporary; it cannot be exchanged for your soul. If you work hard at getting what you want, you might eventually have a "pleasurable" life, but in the end you will find it hollow and empty. Are you willing to make the pursuit of God more important than the selfish pursuits? Follow Jesus, and you will know what it means to live abundantly now and to have eternal life as well.

8:38 Jesus constantly turns the world's perspective upside down with talk of first and last, saving and losing. Here he gives us a choice. We can reject Jesus now and be rejected by him at his second coming, or we can accept him now and be accepted by him then. Rejecting Christ may help us escape shame for the time being, but it will guarantee an eternity of shame later.

9:1 What did Jesus mean when he said that some of the disci-ples would see the Kingdom of God arrive in power? There are

several possibilities. He could have been foretelling his trans-figuration, resurrection and ascension, the coming of the Holy Spirit at Pentecost, or his second coming. The Transfiguration is a strong possibility because Mark immediately tells that story. In the Transfiguration (9:2-8), Peter, James, and John saw Jesus glorified as the Son of God (2 Peter 1:16).

9:2 We don't know why Jesus singled out Peter, James, and John for this special revelation of his glory and purity. Perhaps they were the ones most ready to understand and accept this great truth. These three disciples were the inner circle of the group of 12. They were among the first to hear Jesus' call (1:16-19). They headed the Gospel lists of disciples (3:16). And they were present at certain healings where others were excluded (Luke 8:51).

9:2 Jesus took the disciples to either Mount Hermon or Mount Tabor. A mountain was often associated with closeness to God and readiness to receive his words. God had appeared to both Moses (Exodus 24:12-18) and Elijah (1 Kings 19:8-18) on mountains.

• **9:3ff** The Transfiguration revealed Christ's divine nature. God's voice exalted Jesus above Moses and Elijah as the long-awaited Messiah with full divine authority. Moses represented the law, and Elijah, the prophets. Their appearance showed Jesus as the fulfill-ment of both the Old Testament law and the prophetic promises.

Jesus was not a reincarnation of Elijah or Moses. He was not merely one of the prophets. As God's only Son, he far surpasses them in authority and power. Many voices try to tell us how to live and how to know God personally. Some of these are helpful, many are not. We must first listen to the Bible, and then evaluate all other authorities in light of God's revelation.

• **9:9, 10** Jesus told Peter, James, and John not to speak about what they had seen because they would not fully understand it until Jesus had risen from the dead. Then they would realize that only through dying could Jesus show his power over death and his authority to be King of all. The disciples would not be powerful witnesses for God until they had grasped this truth.

It was natural for the disciples to be confused about Jesus' death and resurrection because they could not see into the future. We, on the other hand, have God's revealed Word, the Bible, to

¹¹Then they asked him, "Why do the teachers of religious law insist that Elijah must return before the Messiah comes?*"

9:13
Ps 22:6-7
Isa 50:6; 53:3
Matt 11:14

¹²Jesus responded, "Elijah is indeed coming first to get everything ready. Yet why do the Scriptures say that the Son of Man must suffer greatly and be treated with utter contempt? ¹³But I tell you, Elijah has already come, and they chose to abuse him, just as the Scriptures predicted."

Jesus Heals a Demon-Possessed Boy (**112**/Matthew 17:14-21; Luke 9:37-43)
¹⁴When they returned to the other disciples, they saw a large crowd surrounding them, and some teachers of religious law were arguing with them. ¹⁵When the crowd saw Jesus, they were overwhelmed with awe, and they ran to greet him.

¹⁶"What is all this arguing about?" Jesus asked.

¹⁷One of the men in the crowd spoke up and said, "Teacher, I brought my son so you could heal him. He is possessed by an evil spirit that won't let him talk. ¹⁸And whenever this spirit seizes him, it throws him violently to the ground. Then he foams at the mouth and grinds his teeth and becomes rigid.* So I asked your disciples to cast out the evil spirit, but they couldn't do it."

¹⁹Jesus said to them,* "You faithless people! How long must I be with you? How long must I put up with you? Bring the boy to me."

9:20
Mark 1:26

²⁰So they brought the boy. But when the evil spirit saw Jesus, it threw the child into a violent convulsion, and he fell to the ground, writhing and foaming at the mouth.

²¹"How long has this been happening?" Jesus asked the boy's father.

He replied, "Since he was a little boy. ²²The spirit often throws him into the fire or into water, trying to kill him. Have mercy on us and help us, if you can."

9:23
Matt 21:21
Mark 11:23-24
Luke 17:6
John 11:40
Acts 14:9

²³"What do you mean, 'If I can'?" Jesus asked. "Anything is possible if a person believes."

²⁴The father instantly cried out, "I do believe, but help me overcome my unbelief!"

9:24
Luke 17:5

²⁵When Jesus saw that the crowd of onlookers was growing, he rebuked the evil* spirit. "Listen, you spirit that makes this boy unable to hear and speak," he said. "I command you to come out of this child and never enter him again!"

9:25
Acts 10:38

²⁶Then the spirit screamed and threw the boy into another violent convulsion and left him. The boy appeared to be dead. A murmur ran through the crowd as people said, "He's dead." ²⁷But Jesus took him by the hand and helped him to his feet, and he stood up.

9:26
Mark 1:26

²⁸Afterward, when Jesus was alone in the house with his disciples, they asked him, "Why couldn't we cast out that evil spirit?"

9:27
Matt 8:15

²⁹Jesus replied, "This kind can be cast out only by prayer.*"

9:11 Greek *that Elijah must come first?* **9:18** Or *becomes weak.* **9:19** Or *said to his disciples.* **9:25** Greek *unclean.* **9:29** Some manuscripts read *by prayer and fasting.*

---

give us the full meaning of Jesus' death and resurrection. We have no excuse for our unbelief.

9:11-13 When Jesus said that Elijah had already come, he was speaking of John the Baptist (Matthew 17:11-13), who had fulfilled the role prophesied for Elijah.

• **9:12, 13** It was difficult for the disciples to grasp the idea that their Messiah would have to suffer. The Jews who studied the Old Testament prophecies expected the Messiah to be a great king like David, who would overthrow the enemy, Rome. Their vision was limited to their own time and experience. They did not understand that the values of God's eternal Kingdom were different from the values of the world. They wanted relief from their present problems, but deliverance from sin is far more important than deliverance from physical suffering or political oppression. Our understanding and appreciation of Jesus must go beyond what he can do for us here and now.

9:18 As the three disciples came down from the mountain with Jesus, they passed from a reassuring experience of God's presence to a frightening experience of evil. The beauty they had just seen must have made the ugliness seem even uglier. As our spiritual vision improves and allows us to see and understand God better, we will also be able to see and understand evil better. We would be overcome by its horror if we did not have Jesus with us to take us through it safely. Don't be afraid to confront evil and suffering, no matter how ugly or horrible. Jesus goes with you.

9:18 Why couldn't the disciples cast out the evil spirit? In 6:13 we read that they cast out demons while on their mission to the villages. Perhaps they had special authority only for that trip, or perhaps their faith was faltering. Mark tells this story to show that the battle with Satan is a difficult, ongoing struggle. Victory over sin and temptation comes through faith in Jesus Christ, not through our own efforts.

9:23 Jesus' words do not mean that we can automatically obtain anything we want if we just think positively. Jesus meant that anything is *possible* if we believe, because nothing is too difficult for God. We cannot have everything we pray for as if by magic, but with faith, we can have everything we need to serve him.

9:24 The attitude of trust and confidence that the Bible calls *belief* or *faith* (Hebrews 11:1, 6) is not something we can obtain without help. Faith is a gift from God (Ephesians 2:8, 9). No matter how much faith we have, we never reach the point of being self-sufficient. Faith is not stored away like money in the bank. Growing in faith is a constant process of daily renewing our trust in Jesus.

9:29 The disciples would often face difficult situations that could be resolved only through prayer. Prayer is the key that unlocks faith in our life. Effective prayer needs both the attitude of complete dependence and the action of asking. Prayer demonstrates our reliance on God as we humbly invite him to fill us with faith and power. There is no substitute for prayer, especially in circumstances that seem impossible.

Jesus Predicts His Death the Second Time (113/Matthew 17:22-23; Luke 9:44-45)

³⁰Leaving that region, they traveled through Galilee. Jesus didn't want anyone to know he was there, ³¹for he wanted to spend more time with his disciples and teach them. He said to them, "The Son of Man is going to be betrayed into the hands of his enemies. He will be killed, but three days later he will rise from the dead." ³²They didn't understand what he was saying, however, and they were afraid to ask him what he meant.

9:31
Matt 16:21
Mark 8:31
Luke 9:22

The Disciples Argue about Who Would Be the Greatest (115/Matthew 18:1-6; Luke 9:46-48)

³³After they arrived at Capernaum and settled in a house, Jesus asked his disciples, "What were you discussing out on the road?" ³⁴But they didn't answer, because they had been arguing about which of them was the greatest. ³⁵He sat down, called the twelve disciples over to him, and said, "Whoever wants to be first must take last place and be the servant of everyone else."

9:34
Luke 22:24
9:35
Matt 20:27

³⁶Then he put a little child among them. Taking the child in his arms, he said to them, ³⁷"Anyone who welcomes a little child like this on my behalf* welcomes me, and anyone who welcomes me welcomes not only me but also my Father who sent me."

9:37
Matt 10:40
Luke 10:16
John 13:20

The Disciples Forbid Another to Use Jesus' Name (116/Luke 9:49-50)

³⁸John said to Jesus, "Teacher, we saw someone using your name to cast out demons, but we told him to stop because he wasn't in our group."

9:38-41
Num 11:26-29
9:39
1 Cor 12:3

³⁹"Don't stop him!" Jesus said. "No one who performs a miracle in my name will soon be able to speak evil of me. ⁴⁰Anyone who is not against us is for us. ⁴¹If anyone gives you even a cup of water because you belong to the Messiah, I tell you the truth, that person will surely be rewarded.

9:40
Matt 12:30
Luke 11:23
9:41
Matt 10:42

Jesus Warns against Temptation (117/Matthew 18:7-9)

⁴²"But if you cause one of these little ones who trusts in me to fall into sin, it would be better for you to be thrown into the sea with a large millstone hung around your neck. ⁴³If your hand causes you to sin, cut it off. It's better to enter eternal life with only one hand than to go into the unquenchable fires of hell* with two hands.* ⁴⁵If your foot causes you to sin, cut it

9:43
Matt 5:30; 18:8

9:37 Greek *in my name.* **9:43a** Greek *Gehenna;* also in 9:45, 47. **9:43b** Some manuscripts add verse 44, *'where the maggots never die and the fire never goes out.'* See 9:48.

9:30, 31 Leaving Caesarea Philippi, Jesus began his last tour through the region of Galilee.

• **9:34** The disciples, caught up in their constant struggle for personal success, were embarrassed to answer Jesus' question. It is always painful to compare our motives with Christ's. It is not wrong for believers to be industrious or ambitious, but when ambition pushes aside obedience and service, it becomes sin. We are all like the disciples and even like the Pharisees in this regard. Pride or insecurity can cause us to overvalue position and prestige. In God's Kingdom, such motives are destructive. The only safe ambition is directed toward Christ's Kingdom, not our own advancement. We must renounce pride and status seeking. They are Satan's tools, not Christ's.

9:35 Serving others is real leadership. Jesus described leadership from a new perspective. Instead of *using* people, we are to *serve* them. Jesus' mission was to serve others and to give his life away. A real leader has a servant's heart. Servant leaders appreciate others' worth and realize that they're not above any job. If you see something that needs to be done, don't wait to be asked; take the initiative and do it like a faithful servant. Don't approach life expecting high positions, honors, and special privileges. Look instead for ways to help others.

9:36, 37 Jesus taught the disciples to welcome children. This was a new approach in a society where children were usually treated as second-class citizens. It is important not only to treat children well but also to teach them about Jesus. Children's ministries should never be regarded as less important than those for adults.

9:38-40 Jesus was not saying that being indifferent or neutral toward him is as good as being committed. As he explained in Matthew 12:30, "Anyone who isn't with me opposes me, and

anyone who isn't working with me is actually working against me." In both cases, Jesus was pointing out that neutrality toward him is not possible. Nevertheless his followers will not all resemble each other or belong to the same groups. People who are on Jesus' side have the same goal of building up the Kingdom of God, and they should not let their differences interfere with this goal. Those who share a common faith in Christ should cooperate. People don't have to be just like us to be following Jesus with us.

• **9:41, 42** Luke 9:48 states, "Whoever is the least among you is the greatest." In Jesus' eyes, whoever welcomes a child welcomes Jesus; giving a cup of cold water to a person in need is the same as giving an offering to God. By contrast, harming others or failing to care for them is a sin, even if they are unimportant people in the world's eyes. It is possible for thoughtless, selfish people to gain a measure of worldly greatness, but lasting greatness is measured by God's standards. What do you use as your measure—personal achievement or unselfish service?

9:42 This caution against harming little ones in the faith applies both to what we do individually as teachers and examples and to what we allow to fester in our Christian fellowship. Our thoughts and actions must be motivated by love (1 Corinthians 13), and we must be careful about judging others (Matthew 7:1-5; Romans 14:1–15:4). However, we also have a responsibility to confront flagrant sin within the church (1 Corinthians 5:12, 13).

9:43ff This startling language is not meant to promote self-mutilation, but instead stresses the importance of cutting sin out of your life. Painful self-discipline is required of his true followers. Giving up a relationship, job, or habit that is against God's will may seem just as painful as cutting off a hand, but Christ is worth any possible loss or discomfort. Nothing should stand in the way of faith. We must be ruthless in removing sin

9:47
Matt 5:29

off. It's better to enter eternal life with only one foot than to be thrown into hell with two feet.* ⁴⁷And if your eye causes you to sin, gouge it out. It's better to enter the Kingdom of God with only one eye than to have two eyes and be thrown into hell, ⁴⁸'where the maggots never die and the fire never goes out.'*

9:50
Matt 5:13
Luke 14:34
Rom 12:18
Col 4:6

⁴⁹"For everyone will be tested with fire.* ⁵⁰Salt is good for seasoning. But if it loses its flavor, how do you make it salty again? You must have the qualities of salt among yourselves and live in peace with each other."

Jesus Teaches about Marriage and Divorce (173/Matthew 19:1-12)

10 Then Jesus left Capernaum and went down to the region of Judea and into the area east of the Jordan River. Once again crowds gathered around him, and as usual he was teaching them.

²Some Pharisees came and tried to trap him with this question: "Should a man be allowed to divorce his wife?"

³Jesus answered them with a question: "What did Moses say in the law about divorce?"

10:4
†Deut 24:1-3

⁴"Well, he permitted it," they replied. "He said a man can give his wife a written notice of divorce and send her away."*

10:6
†Gen 1:27; 5:2

10:7-8
†Gen 2:24
1 Cor 6:16
Eph 5:31

⁵But Jesus responded, "He wrote this commandment only as a concession to your hard hearts. ⁶But 'God made them male and female'* from the beginning of creation. ⁷'This explains why a man leaves his father and mother and is joined to his wife,* ⁸and the two are united into one.'* Since they are no longer two but one, ⁹let no one split apart what God has joined together."

9:45 Some manuscripts add verse 46, *'where the maggots never die and the fire never goes out.'* See 9:48.
9:48 Isa 66:24.   **9:49** Greek *salted with fire;* other manuscripts add *and every sacrifice will be salted with salt.*
10:4 See Deut 24:1.   **10:6** Gen 1:27; 5:2.   **10:7** Some manuscripts do not include *and is joined to his wife.*
10:7-8 Gen 2:24.

---

from our lives now in order to avoid suffering for eternity. Make your choices from an eternal perspective.

9:50 Jesus used salt to illustrate three qualities that should be found in his people: (1) *We should remember God's faithfulness,* just as salt when used with a sacrifice recalled God's covenant with his people (Leviticus 2:13). (2) *We should make a difference in the "flavor" of the world we live in,* just as salt changes meat's flavor (see Matthew 5:13). (3) *We should counteract the moral decay in society,* just as salt preserves food from decay. When we lose this desire to "salt" the earth with the love and message of God, we become useless to him.

10:2 The Pharisees were trying to trap Jesus with their question. If he supported divorce, he would be upholding the Pharisees' procedures, and they doubted that he would do that. If Jesus spoke against divorce, however, some members of the crowd would dislike his position; some may have even used the law to their advantage to divorce their wives. More important, he might incur the wrath of Herod, who had already killed John the Baptist for speaking out against divorce and adultery (6:17-28). This is what the Pharisees wanted.

The Pharisees saw divorce as a legal issue rather than a spiritual one. Jesus used this test as an opportunity to review God's intended purpose for marriage and to expose the Pharisees' selfish motives. They were not thinking about what God intended for marriage and were quoting Moses unfairly and out of context. Jesus showed these legal experts how superficial their knowledge really was.

10:5-9 God allowed divorce as a concession to people's sinfulness. Unfortunately, the Pharisees used Deuteronomy 24:1 as a proof text for the sanctioning of divorce. Jesus explained that divorce was not God's ideal; instead, God wants married people to consider their marriage permanent. Don't enter marriage with the option of getting out. Your marriage is more likely to be happy if from the outset you are committed to permanence. Don't be hardhearted like these Pharisees, but be hardheaded in your determination, with God's help, to stay together.

That said, we know that in our world, divorce is sometimes necessary (for physical survival, for well-being of children, etc.). Jesus clearly gave God's ideal for marriage in Genesis priority

over Moses' permission for divorce. Jesus did not cancel Moses' teaching, however. For possible exceptions, see Matthew 5:32 and 19:9, where Jesus permitted divorce when the spouse had been unfaithful; and 1 Corinthians 7:15, where Paul recognized divorce when the unbelieving partner leaves the marriage. Divorce is wrong; it severs a holy union. But divorce is permitted. Jesus did not elaborate on the permissible reasons, but his high view of marriage surely requires that divorce be a last resort to avoid greater disaster.

10:6-9 Women were often treated as property. Marriage and divorce were regarded as transactions similar to buying and selling land. But Jesus condemned this attitude, clarifying God's original intention—that marriage bring oneness (Genesis 2:24). Jesus held up God's ideal for marriage and told his followers to live by that ideal.

FINAL TRIP TO JUDEA
Jesus quietly left Capernaum, heading toward the borders of Judea before crossing the Jordan River. He preached there before going to Jericho. This trip from Galilee was his last; he would not return before his death.

¹⁰Later, when he was alone with his disciples in the house, they brought up the subject again. ¹¹He told them, "Whoever divorces his wife and marries someone else commits adultery against her. ¹²And if a woman divorces her husband and marries someone else, she commits adultery."

10:11
Matt 5:32
Luke 16:18
1 Cor 7:10-11

Jesus Blesses the Children (174/Matthew 19:13-15; Luke 18:15-17)

¹³One day some parents brought their children to Jesus so he could touch and bless them. But the disciples scolded the parents for bothering him.

¹⁴When Jesus saw what was happening, he was angry with his disciples. He said to them, "Let the children come to me. Don't stop them! For the Kingdom of God belongs to those who are like these children. ¹⁵I tell you the truth, anyone who doesn't receive the Kingdom of God like a child will never enter it." ¹⁶Then he took the children in his arms and placed his hands on their heads and blessed them.

10:15
Matt 18:3
10:16
Mark 9:36

Jesus Speaks to the Rich Young Man (175/Matthew 19:16-30; Luke 18:18-30)

¹⁷As Jesus was starting out on his way to Jerusalem, a man came running up to him, knelt down, and asked, "Good Teacher, what must I do to inherit eternal life?"

¹⁸"Why do you call me good?" Jesus asked. "Only God is truly good. ¹⁹But to answer your question, you know the commandments: 'You must not murder. You must not commit adultery. You must not steal. You must not testify falsely. You must not cheat anyone. Honor your father and mother.'*"

10:19
†Exod 20:12-16
†Deut 5:16-20
Rom 13:9

²⁰"Teacher," the man replied, "I've obeyed all these commandments since I was young."

²¹Looking at the man, Jesus felt genuine love for him. "There is still one thing you haven't done," he told him. "Go and sell all your possessions and give the money to the poor, and you will have treasure in heaven. Then come, follow me."

10:21
Matt 6:19-20
Luke 12:33
Acts 2:44-45

²²At this the man's face fell, and he went away sad, for he had many possessions.

²³Jesus looked around and said to his disciples, "How hard it is for the rich to enter the Kingdom of God!" ²⁴This amazed them. But Jesus said again, "Dear children, it is very hard* to enter the Kingdom of God. ²⁵In fact, it is easier for a camel to go through the eye of a needle than for a rich person to enter the Kingdom of God!"

10:24
Matt 7:13-14
John 3:5

10:19 Exod 20:12-16; Deut 5:16-20. **10:24** Some manuscripts read *very hard for those who trust in riches.*

• **10:13-16** Jesus was often criticized for spending too much time with the wrong people—children, tax collectors, and sinners (Matthew 9:11; Luke 15:1, 2; 19:7). Some, including the disciples, thought Jesus should be spending more time with important leaders and the devout because this was the way to improve his position and avoid criticism. But Jesus didn't need to improve his position. He was God, and he wanted to speak to those who needed him most.

10:14 To feel secure, all children need is a loving look and gentle touch from someone who cares. They believe us because they trust us. Jesus said that people should trust in him with this kind of childlike faith. We do not have to understand all the mysteries of the universe; it should be enough to know that God loves us and provides forgiveness for our sin.

10:15 How can you "receive the Kingdom of God like a child"? Adults considering the Christian faith for the first time will have life experiences that take them way past the ability to be as innocent as children. Jesus does not ask us to put aside our experiences, but he does require a change of attitude: adult self-sufficiency must recognize its need for the sovereign God; and adult moral defensiveness must humble itself before the holy God; and adult skeptical toughness must soften before the loving God. Children do not feel supremely powerful, perfectly righteous, or totally autonomous. These are adult fantasies. Coming to Jesus means to accept his goodness on your behalf, confess your need, and commit your life to his tender guidance.

• **10:17-23** This man wanted to be sure he would get eternal life, so he asked what he could *do.* He said he'd never once broken any of the laws Jesus mentioned (10:19), and perhaps he had even kept the Pharisees' additional regulations as well. But Jesus lovingly broke through the man's pride with a challenge that brought out his true motives: "Go and sell all your possessions and give the money to the poor." This challenge exposed the barrier that could

keep this man out of the Kingdom: his love of money. Money represented his pride of accomplishment and self-effort. Ironically, his attitude made him unable to keep the first commandment: to let nothing be more important than God (Exodus 20:3). He could not meet the one requirement Jesus gave—to turn his whole heart and life over to God. The man came to Jesus wondering what he could do; he left seeing what he was unable to do. What barriers are keeping you from turning your life over to Christ?

10:18 When Jesus asked this question, he was saying, "Do you really know the one to whom you are talking?" Because only God is truly good, the man was calling Jesus "God," whether or not he realized it.

10:21 What does your money mean to you? Although Jesus wanted this man to sell everything and give his money to the poor, this does not mean that all believers should sell all their possessions. Most of his followers did not sell everything, although they used their possessions to serve others. Instead, this incident shows us that we must not let our possessions or money keep us from following Jesus. We must remove all barriers to serving him fully. If Jesus asked, could you give up your house? your car? your level of income? your position on the ladder of promotion? Your reaction may show your attitude toward money—whether it is your servant or your master.

10:21 Jesus showed genuine love for this man, even though he knew that the man might not follow him. Love is able to give tough advice; it doesn't hedge on the truth. Christ loved us enough to die for us, and he also loves us enough to talk straight to us. If his love were superficial, he would give us only his approval; but because his love is complete, he gives us life-changing challenges.

10:23 Jesus said it was very difficult for the rich to enter the Kingdom of God because the rich, having their basic physical needs met, often become self-reliant. When they feel empty, they buy something new to try to fill the void that only God can fill.

²⁶The disciples were astounded. "Then who in the world can be saved?" they asked.

10:27
Gen 18:14
Job 42:2
Mark 14:36

²⁷Jesus looked at them intently and said, "Humanly speaking, it is impossible. But not with God. Everything is possible with God."

²⁸Then Peter began to speak up. "We've given up everything to follow you," he said.

10:28
Mark 1:18

²⁹"Yes," Jesus replied, "and I assure you that everyone who has given up house or brothers or sisters or mother or father or children or property, for my sake and for the Good News,

10:30
2 Tim 3:12

³⁰will receive now in return a hundred times as many houses, brothers, sisters, mothers, children, and property—along with persecution. And in the world to come that person will

10:31
Matt 20:16
Luke 13:30

have eternal life. ³¹But many who are the greatest now will be least important then, and those who seem least important now will be the greatest then.*"

Jesus Predicts His Death the Third Time (**177**/Matthew 20:17-19; Luke 18:31-34)

³²They were now on the way up to Jerusalem, and Jesus was walking ahead of them. The disciples were filled with awe, and the people following behind were overwhelmed with fear.

10:33
Matt 16:21;
17:22-23
Mark 8:31; 9:31
Luke 24:7

10:34
Isa 50:6

Taking the twelve disciples aside, Jesus once more began to describe everything that was about to happen to him. ³³"Listen," he said, "we're going up to Jerusalem, where the Son of Man* will be betrayed to the leading priests and the teachers of religious law. They will sentence him to die and hand him over to the Romans.* ³⁴They will mock him, spit on him, flog him with a whip, and kill him, but after three days he will rise again."

Jesus Teaches about Serving Others (**178**/Matthew 20:20-28)

³⁵Then James and John, the sons of Zebedee, came over and spoke to him. "Teacher," they said, "we want you to do us a favor."

³⁶"What is your request?" he asked.

³⁷They replied, "When you sit on your glorious throne, we want to sit in places of honor next to you, one on your right and the other on your left."

10:38
Luke 12:50
John 18:11

³⁸But Jesus said to them, "You don't know what you are asking! Are you able to drink from the bitter cup of suffering I am about to drink? Are you able to be baptized with the baptism of suffering I must be baptized with?"

³⁹"Oh yes," they replied, "we are able!"

10:39
Acts 12:2
Rev 1:9

Then Jesus told them, "You will indeed drink from my bitter cup and be baptized with my baptism of suffering. ⁴⁰But I have no right to say who will sit on my right or my left. God has prepared those places for the ones he has chosen."

⁴¹When the ten other disciples heard what James and John had asked, they were indignant.

10:31 Greek *But many who are first will be last; and the last, first.*   **10:33a** "Son of Man" is a title Jesus used for himself.   **10:33b** Greek *the Gentiles.*

Their abundance and self-sufficiency become their deficiency. The person who has everything on earth can still lack what is most important—eternal life.

10:26 The disciples were amazed. Was not wealth a blessing from God, a reward for being good? This misconception is still common today. Although many believers enjoy material prosperity, many others live in poverty. Wealth is not a sign of faith or of partiality on God's part.

10:29, 30 Jesus assured the disciples that anyone who gives up something valuable for his sake will be repaid a hundred times over in this life, although not necessarily in the same way. For example, someone may be rejected by his family for accepting Christ, but he or she will gain the larger family of believers. Along with these rewards, however, we experience persecution because the world hates God. Jesus emphasized persecution to make sure that people do not selfishly follow him only for the rewards.

10:31 Jesus explained that in the world to come, the values of this world will be reversed. Those who seek status and importance here will have none in heaven. Those who are humble here will be great in heaven. The corrupt condition of our society encourages confusion in values. We are bombarded by messages that tell us how to be important and how to feel good, and Jesus' teaching about service to others seems alien. But those who have humbly served others are most qualified to be great in heaven.

10:33, 34 Jesus' death and resurrection should have come as no surprise to the disciples. Here he clearly explained to them what would happen to him. Unfortunately, they didn't really hear what

he was saying. Jesus said he was the Messiah, but they thought the Messiah would be a conquering king. He spoke to them of resurrection, but they heard only his words about death. Because Jesus often spoke in parables, the disciples may have thought that his words on death and resurrection were another parable they weren't astute enough to understand. Jesus' predictions of his death and resurrection show that these events were God's plan from the beginning and not accidents.

10:35 Mark records that John and James went to Jesus with their request; in Matthew, their mother also made the request. Apparently mother and sons were in agreement in requesting honored places in Christ's Kingdom.

• **10:37** The disciples, like most Jews of that day, had the wrong idea of the Messiah's Kingdom as predicted by the Old Testament prophets. They thought Jesus would establish an earthly kingdom that would free Israel from Rome's oppression. James and John wanted honored places in it. But Jesus' Kingdom is not of this world; it is not centered in palaces and thrones but in the hearts and lives of his followers. The disciples did not understand this until after Jesus' resurrection.

10:38, 39 James and John said they were willing to face any trial for Christ. Both did suffer: James died as a martyr (Acts 12:2), and John was forced to live in exile (Revelation 1:9). It is easy to say we will endure anything for Christ, and yet most of us complain about the most minor problems. We may say that we are willing to suffer for Christ, but are we willing to suffer the minor irritations that sometimes come with serving others?

⁴²So Jesus called them together and said, "You know that the rulers in this world lord it over their people, and officials flaunt their authority over those under them. ⁴³But among you it will be different. Whoever wants to be a leader among you must be your servant, ⁴⁴and whoever wants to be first among you must be the slave of everyone else. ⁴⁵For even the Son of Man came not to be served but to serve others and to give his life as a ransom for many."

Jesus Heals a Blind Beggar (**179**/Matthew 20:29-34; Luke 18:35-43)
⁴⁶Then they reached Jericho, and as Jesus and his disciples left town, a large crowd followed him. A blind beggar named Bartimaeus (son of Timaeus) was sitting beside the road. ⁴⁷When Bartimaeus heard that Jesus of Nazareth was nearby, he began to shout, "Jesus, Son of David, have mercy on me!"

⁴⁸"Be quiet!" many of the people yelled at him.

But he only shouted louder, "Son of David, have mercy on me!"

⁴⁹When Jesus heard him, he stopped and said, "Tell him to come here."

So they called the blind man. "Cheer up," they said. "Come on, he's calling you!" ⁵⁰Bartimaeus threw aside his coat, jumped up, and came to Jesus.

⁵¹"What do you want me to do for you?" Jesus asked.

"My rabbi,*" the blind man said, "I want to see!"

⁵²And Jesus said to him, "Go, for your faith has healed you." Instantly the man could see, and he followed Jesus down the road.*

3. Jesus' ministry in Jerusalem
Jesus Rides into Jerusalem on a Young Donkey
(**183**/Matthew 21:1-11; Luke 19:28-44; John 12:12-19)

11 As Jesus and his disciples approached Jerusalem, they came to the towns of Bethphage and Bethany on the Mount of Olives. Jesus sent two of them on ahead. ²"Go into that

10:51 Greek uses the Hebrew term *Rabboni*.   **10:52** Or *on the way.*

Cross references (right margin):
10:42 Luke 22:25-27; 1 Pet 5:3
10:43-44 Matt 23:11; Mark 9:35; Luke 22:26
10:45 Matt 20:28; John 13:14; Phil 2:7; 1 Tim 2:5-6; Titus 2:14
10:47 Isa 11:1; Jer 23:5-6; Matt 9:27; 15:22
10:52 Matt 9:22; Mark 5:34; Luke 7:50; 8:48; 17:19
11:2 1 Sam 6:7; Zech 9:9

• **10:42-45** James and John wanted the highest positions in Jesus' Kingdom. But Jesus told them that true greatness comes in serving others. Peter, one of the disciples who had heard this message, expands the thought in 1 Peter 5:1-4.

Businesses, organizations, and institutions measure greatness by personal achievement. In Christ's Kingdom, however, service is the way to get ahead. The desire to be on top will hinder, not help. Rather than seeking to have your needs met, look for ways that you can minister to the needs of others.

10:45 This verse reveals not only the motive for Jesus' ministry but also the basis for our salvation. A ransom was the price paid to release a slave. Jesus paid a ransom for us because we could not pay it ourselves. His death released all of us from our slavery to sin. The disciples thought Jesus' life and power would save them from Rome; Jesus said his *death* would save them from sin,

an even greater slavery than Rome's. More about the ransom Jesus paid for us is found in 1 Peter 1:18, 19.

10:46 Jericho was a popular resort city rebuilt by Herod the Great in the Judean desert, not far from the Jordan River crossing. Jesus was on his way to Jerusalem (10:32), and, after crossing over from Perea, he would naturally enter Jericho.

10:46 Beggars were a common sight in most towns. Because most occupations of that day required physical labor, anyone with a crippling disease or disability was at a severe disadvantage and was usually forced to beg, even though God's laws commanded care for such needy people (Leviticus 25:35-38). Blindness was considered a curse from God for sin (John 9:2), but Jesus refuted this idea when he reached out to heal the blind.

• **10:47** "Son of David" was a popular way of addressing Jesus as the Messiah, because it was known that the Messiah would be a descendant of King David (Isaiah 9:7). The fact that Bartimaeus called Jesus the Son of David shows that he recognized Jesus as the Messiah. His faith in Jesus as the Messiah brought about his healing.

10:47 We do not know how long Bartimaeus had been blind, but it only took a moment for him to decide to call on Jesus for help. Jesus met many spiritually blind people—religious leaders, family members, people in the crowd. Though their eyes were fine, they could not see the truth about Jesus. But blind Bartimaeus heard the report that Jesus was coming and boldly cried out.

In coming to Jesus, we need Bartimaeus's boldness. We must overcome our reticence and doubts and take the step to call on him. Bartimaeus had not seen Jesus' miracles, but he responded in faith to what he had heard. We have heard Jesus described in the Gospels. May we be like those of whom Peter wrote, "You love him even though you have never seen him. Though you do not see him now, you trust him; and you rejoice with a glorious, inexpressible joy" (1 Peter 1:8).

• **11:1, 2** This was Sunday of the week that Jesus would be crucified, and the great Passover festival was about to begin. Jews came to Jerusalem from all over the Roman world during this week-long celebration to remember the great exodus from Egypt

JESUS NEARS JERUSALEM
Leaving Jericho, Jesus headed toward acclaim, then crucifixion, in Jerusalem. During his last week, he stayed outside the city in Bethany, a village on the eastern slope of the Mount of Olives, entering Jerusalem to teach, eat the Passover, and finally be crucified.

village over there," he told them. "As soon as you enter it, you will see a young donkey tied there that no one has ever ridden. Untie it and bring it here. ³If anyone asks, 'What are you doing?' just say, 'The Lord needs it and will return it soon.'"

⁴The two disciples left and found the colt standing in the street, tied outside the front door. ⁵As they were untying it, some bystanders demanded, "What are you doing, untying that colt?" ⁶They said what Jesus had told them to say, and they were permitted to take it. ⁷Then they brought the colt to Jesus and threw their garments over it, and he sat on it.

⁸Many in the crowd spread their garments on the road ahead of him, and others spread leafy branches they had cut in the fields. ⁹Jesus was in the center of the procession, and the people all around him were shouting,

11:9-10
†Pss 118:25-26;
148:1

"Praise God!*
Blessings on the one who comes in the name of the Lᴏʀᴅ!
¹⁰ Blessings on the coming Kingdom of our ancestor David!
Praise God in highest heaven!"*

11:11
Matt 21:10, 17

¹¹So Jesus came to Jerusalem and went into the Temple. After looking around carefully at everything, he left because it was late in the afternoon. Then he returned to Bethany with the twelve disciples.

11:9 Greek *Hosanna*, an exclamation of praise that literally means "save now"; also in 11:10.
11:9-10 Pss 118:25-26; 148:1.

KEY CHARACTER-ISTICS OF CHRIST IN THE GOSPELS

Characteristic	Reference
Jesus is the Son of God.	Matthew 16:15, 16; Mark 1:1; Luke 22:70, 71; John 8:24
Jesus is God who became human.	John 1:1, 2, 14; 20:28
Jesus is the Christ, the Messiah	Matthew 26:63, 64; Mark 14:61, 62; Luke 9:20; John 4:25, 26
Jesus came to help sinners	Matthew 9:13; Luke 5:32
Jesus has power to forgive sins.	Mark 2:9-12; Luke 24:47
Jesus has authority over death	Matthew 28:5, 6; Mark 5:22-24, 35-42; Luke 24:5, 6; John 11:1-44
Jesus has power to give eternal life.	John 10:28; 17:2
Jesus healed the sick.	Matthew 8:5-13; Mark 1:32-34; Luke 5:12-15; John 9:1-7
Jesus taught with authority	Matthew 7:29; Mark 1:21, 22
Jesus was compassionate.	Matthew 9:36; Mark 1:41; 8:2
Jesus experienced sorrow	Matthew 26:38; John 11:35
Jesus never disobeyed God.	Matthew 3:15; John 8:46

(see Exodus 12:37-51). Many in the crowds had heard of or seen Jesus and were hoping he would come to the Temple (John 11:55-57).

Jesus did come, not as a warring king on a horse or in a chariot, but as a gentle and peaceable King on a donkey's colt, just as Zechariah 9:9 had predicted. Jesus knew that those who would hear him teach at the Temple would return to their homes throughout the world and announce the coming of the Messiah.

• **11:9, 10** The people exclaimed "Praise God!" because they recognized that Jesus was fulfilling the prophecy in Zechariah 9:9 (see also Psalms 24:7-10; 118:26). They spoke of David's king-dom because of God's words to David in 2 Samuel 7:12-14. The crowd correctly saw Jesus as the fulfillment of these prophecies, but they did not understand where Jesus' kingship would lead him. This same crowd cried out, "Crucify him!" when Jesus stood on trial only a few days later.

11:10 Like those who witnessed Jesus' victory parade into Jerusalem, we have expectations for what we think God should do to make life better, safer, and more enjoyable. Like excited spectators, we can't wait to see suffering stopped, injustice corrected, and prosperity begun. Like the people on the road

to Jerusalem that day, we have much to learn about Jesus' death and resurrection. We must not let our personal desires catch us up in the celebration and shouting lest we miss the meaning of true discipleship. In our excitement and celebration, we must remember that following Christ involves hardships. It may include suffering, even death.

11:11-21 In this passage, two unusual incidents are related: the cursing of the fig tree and the clearing of the Temple. The cursing of the fig tree was an acted-out parable related to the clearing of the Temple. The Temple was supposed to be a place of worship, but true worship had disappeared. The fig tree showed promise of fruit, but it produced none. Jesus was show-ing his anger at religious life without substance. If you claim to have faith without putting it to work in your life, you are like the barren fig tree. Genuine faith has great potential; ask God to help you bear fruit for his Kingdom.

Jesus Clears the Temple Again (**184**/Matthew 21:12-17; Luke 19:45-48)

¹²The next morning as they were leaving Bethany, Jesus was hungry. ¹³He noticed a fig tree in full leaf a little way off, so he went over to see if he could find any figs. But there were only leaves because it was too early in the season for fruit. ¹⁴Then Jesus said to the tree, "May no one ever eat your fruit again!" And the disciples heard him say it.

¹⁵When they arrived back in Jerusalem, Jesus entered the Temple and began to drive out the people buying and selling animals for sacrifices. He knocked over the tables of the money changers and the chairs of those selling doves, ¹⁶and he stopped everyone from using the Temple as a marketplace.* ¹⁷He said to them, "The Scriptures declare, 'My Temple will be called a house of prayer for all nations,' but you have turned it into a den of thieves.'"*

11:17
†Isa 56:7
†Jer 7:11

¹⁸When the leading priests and teachers of religious law heard what Jesus had done, they began planning how to kill him. But they were afraid of him because the people were so amazed at his teaching.

11:18
Matt 21:46
Mark 12:12
Luke 20:19

¹⁹That evening Jesus and the disciples left* the city.

Jesus Says the Disciples Can Pray for Anything (**188**/Matthew 21:18-22)

²⁰The next morning as they passed by the fig tree he had cursed, the disciples noticed it had withered from the roots up. ²¹Peter remembered what Jesus had said to the tree on the previous day and exclaimed, "Look, Rabbi! The fig tree you cursed has withered and died!"

²²Then Jesus said to the disciples, "Have faith in God. ²³I tell you the truth, you can say to this mountain, 'May you be lifted up and thrown into the sea,' and it will happen. But you must really believe it will happen and have no doubt in your heart. ²⁴I tell you, you can pray for anything, and if you believe that you've received it, it will be yours. ²⁵But when you are praying, first forgive anyone you are holding a grudge against, so that your Father in heaven will forgive your sins, too.*"

11:22
Matt 17:20
Luke 17:6

11:24
Matt 7:7

11:25
Matt 5:23; 6:14

11:16 Or *from carrying merchandise through the Temple.* **11:17** Isa 56:7; Jer 7:11. **11:19** Greek *they left;* other manuscripts read *he left.* **11:25** Some manuscripts add verse 26, *But if you refuse to forgive, your Father in heaven will not forgive your sins.* Compare Matt 6:15.

11:13-26 Fig trees, a popular source of inexpensive food in Israel, require three years from the time they are planted until they can bear fruit. Each tree yields a great amount of fruit twice a year, in late spring and in early autumn. This incident occurred early in the spring when the leaves were beginning to bud. The figs normally grow as the leaves fill out, but this tree, though full of leaves, had no figs. The tree looked promising but offered no fruit. Jesus' harsh words to the fig tree could be applied to the nation of Israel. Fruitful in appearance only, Israel was spiritually barren.

11:15-17 Jesus became angry, but he did not sin. There is a place for righteous indignation. Christians are right to be upset about sin and injustice and should take a stand against them. Unfortunately, believers are often passive about these important issues and instead get angry over personal insults and petty irritations. Make sure your anger is directed toward the right issues.

• **11:15-17** Money changers and merchants did big business during Passover. Those who came from foreign countries had to have their money changed into Temple currency because this was the only money accepted for the Temple tax and for the purchase of sacrificial animals. Often the inflated exchange rate enriched the money changers, and the exorbitant prices of animals made the merchants wealthy. Their stalls were set up in the Temple's Court of the Gentiles, making it all but impossible for non-Jews to spend any time in worship (Isaiah 56:6, 7). Jesus became angry because God's house of worship had become a place of extortion and a barrier to Gentiles who wanted to worship.

• **11:22, 23** The kind of prayer that moves mountains is prayer for the fruitfulness of God's Kingdom. It would seem impossible to move a mountain into the sea, so Jesus used that illustration to show that God can do the impossible. God will answer your prayers but not as a result of your positive mental attitude. Other conditions must be met: (1) You must be a believer; (2) you must not hold a grudge against another person; (3) you must not pray with selfish motives; (4) your request must be for the good of God's Kingdom. To pray effectively, you need faith in God, not faith in the object of your request. If you focus only on your request, you will be left with nothing if your request is refused.

11:24 Jesus, our example, prayed, "Everything is possible for you. . . . Yet I want your will to be done, not mine" (14:36). Our prayers are often motivated by our own interests and desires. We like to hear that we can have anything. But Jesus prayed with

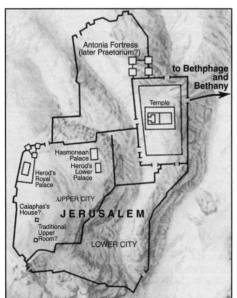

CLEARING THE TEMPLE On Monday morning of his last week, Jesus left Bethany, entered Jerusalem, and cleared the Temple of money changers and merchants.

Antonia Fortress
(later Praetorium?)

to Bethphage
and
Bethany

Temple

Hasmonean
Palace
Herod's
Lower
Palace
Herod's
Royal
Palace

UPPER CITY

Caiaphas's
House?

JERUSALEM

Traditional
Upper
Room?

LOWER CITY

Religious Leaders Challenge Jesus' Authority (**189**/Matthew 21:23-27; Luke 20:1-8)

27Again they entered Jerusalem. As Jesus was walking through the Temple area, the leading priests, the teachers of religious law, and the elders came up to him. 28They demanded, "By what authority are you doing all these things? Who gave you the right to do them?"

29"I'll tell you by what authority I do these things if you answer one question," Jesus replied. 30"Did John's authority to baptize come from heaven, or was it merely human? Answer me!"

31They talked it over among themselves. "If we say it was from heaven, he will ask why we didn't believe John. 32But do we dare say it was merely human?" For they were afraid of what the people would do, because everyone believed that John was a prophet. 33So they finally replied, "We don't know."

And Jesus responded, "Then I won't tell you by what authority I do these things."

Jesus Tells the Parable of the Evil Farmers (**191**/Matthew 21:33-46; Luke 20:9-19)

12 Then Jesus began teaching them with stories: "A man planted a vineyard. He built a wall around it, dug a pit for pressing out the grape juice, and built a lookout tower. Then he leased the vineyard to tenant farmers and moved to another country. 2At the time of the grape harvest, he sent one of his servants to collect his share of the crop. 3But the farmers grabbed the servant, beat him up, and sent him back empty-handed. 4The owner then sent another servant, but they insulted him and beat him over the head. 5The next servant he sent was killed. Others he sent were either beaten or killed, 6until there was only one left—his son whom he loved dearly. The owner finally sent him, thinking, 'Surely they will respect my son.'

7"But the tenant farmers said to one another, 'Here comes the heir to this estate. Let's kill him and get the estate for ourselves!' 8So they grabbed him and murdered him and threw his body out of the vineyard.

9"What do you suppose the owner of the vineyard will do?" Jesus asked. "I'll tell you—he will come and kill those farmers and lease the vineyard to others. 10Didn't you ever read this in the Scriptures?

'The stone that the builders rejected
    has now become the cornerstone.
11 This is the LORD's doing,
    and it is wonderful to see.'*"

12The religious leaders* wanted to arrest Jesus because they realized he was telling the story against them—they were the wicked farmers. But they were afraid of the crowd, so they left him and went away.

12:10-11 Ps 118:22-23. **12:12** Greek *They.*

Marginal references:

11:32
Matt 14:5; 21:46

12:1
Isa 5:1-2

12:5
2 Chr 24:21;
36:15-16
Neh 9:26
Matt 23:34-37
Acts 7:52
1 Thes 2:15

12:6
Rom 8:3
Gal 4:4

12:8
Heb 13:12

12:10-11
†Ps 118:22-23
Acts 4:11
Rom 9:33
Eph 2:20
1 Pet 2:5-7

12:12
Mark 11:18

God's interests in mind. When we pray, we can express our desires, but we should want his will above ours. Check yourself to see if your prayers focus on your interests or God's.

11:25 Forgiving others is tough work—so much so that many people would rather do something totally distasteful than offer forgiveness to someone who has wronged them. For a person to pray while bearing a grudge, however, is like a tree sprouting leaves and bearing no fruit (11:13). True faith changes the heart. Real prayer dismantles pride and vengeance, filling the holes with love. Real faith seeks peace. For our churches to have prayer power, there must be harmony and forgiveness evident in the body of believers. Let go of hurts, abandon grudges, and forgive others.

• **11:27-33** The religious leaders were in a quandary. They had wanted to trap Jesus with a question that would show him to be either a blasphemer or a weird fanatic. Instead, Jesus had countered their question with a question about John the Baptist. Now they would have to try to save face. They had not stood up for John or tried to get him released—John had irritated them just as Jesus was doing (see Matthew 3:7-10). Always cloaked in self-interest, these religious leaders were only concerned about position and reputation; they weren't looking for the truth. In John 3:19, Jesus summed up this attitude: "People loved the darkness more than the light, for their actions were evil." People who reject

Jesus' claims have a greater problem than intellectual doubt; they are rebelling against Christ's control of their lives. They try to ask tricky questions, but don't really want an answer. Sincere seekers, however, will find the truth (Matthew 7:7, 8).

11:30 For more information, see John the Baptist's Profile in John 1, p. 1749.

12:1ff In this parable, the man who planted the vineyard is God; the vineyard is the nation Israel; the tenant farmers are Israel's religious leaders; the servants are the prophets and priests who remained faithful to God; the son is Jesus; and the others are the Gentiles. The religious leaders not only frustrated their nation's purpose but also killed those who were trying to fulfill it. They were so jealous and possessive that they ignored the welfare of the very people they were supposed to be bringing to God. By telling this story, Jesus exposed the religious leaders' plot to kill him and warned that their sins would be punished.

12:10, 11 Jesus referred to himself as the stone rejected by the builders. Although he would be rejected by most of the Jewish leaders, he would become the cornerstone of a new "building," the church (Acts 4:11, 12). The cornerstone was used as a base to make sure the other stones of the building were straight and level. Likewise, Jesus' life and teaching would be the church's foundation.

Religious Leaders Question Jesus about Paying Taxes
(**193**/Matthew 22:15-22; Luke 20:20-26)

¹³Later the leaders sent some Pharisees and supporters of Herod to trap Jesus into saying something for which he could be arrested. ¹⁴"Teacher," they said, "we know how honest you are. You are impartial and don't play favorites. You teach the way of God truthfully. Now tell us—is it right to pay taxes to Caesar or not? ¹⁵Should we pay them, or shouldn't we?"

Jesus saw through their hypocrisy and said, "Why are you trying to trap me? Show me a Roman coin,* and I'll tell you." ¹⁶When they handed it to him, he asked, "Whose picture and title are stamped on it?"

"Caesar's," they replied.

¹⁷"Well, then," Jesus said, "give to Caesar what belongs to Caesar, and give to God what belongs to God."

    12:17
    Rom 13:7

His reply completely amazed them.

Religious Leaders Question Jesus about the Resurrection
(**194**/Matthew 22:23-33; Luke 20:27-40)

¹⁸Then Jesus was approached by some Sadducees—religious leaders who say there is no resurrection from the dead. They posed this question: ¹⁹"Teacher, Moses gave us a law that if a man dies, leaving a wife without children, his brother should marry the widow and have a child who will carry on the brother's name.* ²⁰Well, suppose there were seven brothers. The oldest one married and then died without children. ²¹So the second brother married the widow, but he also died without children. Then the third brother married her. ²²This continued with all seven of them, and still there were no children. Last of all, the woman also died. ²³So tell us, whose wife will she be in the resurrection? For all seven were married to her."

    12:18-27
    Acts 23:8
    1 Cor 15:12
    12:19
    †Gen 38:8
    †Deut 25:5

²⁴Jesus replied, "Your mistake is that you don't know the Scriptures, and you don't know the power of God. ²⁵For when the dead rise, they will neither marry nor be given in marriage. In this respect they will be like the angels in heaven.

    12:25
    1 Cor 15:42, 49, 52

12:15 Greek *a denarius*.   **12:19** See Deut 25:5-6.

12:13 The Pharisees were primarily a religious group concerned with ritual purity; the supporters of Herod were a Jewish political group that approved of Herod's compromises with Rome. The Pharisees did not like Jesus because he exposed their hypocrisy. The supporters of Herod also saw Jesus as a threat. Supporters of the dynasty of Herod the Great, they had lost political control when, as a result of reported unrest, Rome deposed Archelaus (Herod's son with authority over Judea), and replaced him with a Roman governor. The supporters of Herod feared that Jesus would cause still more instability in Judea and that Rome might react by never allowing the Roman leaders to step down and be replaced by a descendant of Herod.

• **12:14** Anyone who avoided paying taxes faced harsh penalties. The Jews hated to pay taxes to Rome because the money supported their oppressors and symbolized their subjection. Much of the tax money also went to maintain the pagan temples and luxurious lifestyles of Rome's upper class. The Pharisees and supporters of Herod hoped to trap Jesus with this tax question. A yes would mean he supported Rome, which would turn the people against him. A no would bring accusations of treason and rebellion against Rome and could lead to civil penalties.

• **12:17** Jesus avoided the trick question by showing that believers have dual citizenship (1 Peter 2:17). Our citizenship in the nation requires that we pay money for the services and benefits we receive. Our citizenship in the Kingdom of Heaven requires that we pledge to God our primary obedience and commitment. (See Acts 4:18, 19 and 5:29 for discussions on obeying God rather than people.) As God's followers, we have legitimate obligations to both God and the government. But it is important to keep our priorities straight. When the two authorities conflict, our duty to God always must come before our duty to the government. The coin bearing the emperor's image should be given to the emperor; our lives, bearing God's image, belong to God. Are you giving to God what is rightfully his?

• **12:18-23** After the Pharisees and supporters of Herod failed to trap Jesus with their tax question, the Sadducees stepped in with a question they were sure would stump him. This was a question that they had successfully used against the Pharisees, who could not come up with an answer. The Sadducees did not believe in life after death because the Pentateuch (Genesis—Deuteronomy) had no direct teaching about it, and the writings of Moses were the only Scriptures they followed. But Jesus was about to point out that Moses' books support the idea of eternal life (12:26).

12:19 According to Old Testament law, when a man died without a son, his brother had to marry the widow and produce children to care for her and allow the family line to continue. The first son of this marriage was considered the heir of the dead man (Deuteronomy 25:5, 6).

12:24 What life will be like after the resurrection is far beyond our ability to understand or imagine (Isaiah 64:4; 1 Corinthians 2:9). We need not be afraid of eternal life because of the unknowns, however. Instead of wondering what God's coming Kingdom will be like, we should concentrate on our relationship with Christ right now because in the new Kingdom, we will be with him. If we learn to love and trust Christ *now*, we will not be afraid of what he has in store for us then.

12:25-27 Jesus' statement does not mean that people won't recognize their spouses in the coming Kingdom. It simply means that God's new order will not be an extension of this life and that the same physical and natural rules won't apply. Jesus' comment in verse 25 was not intended to be the final word on marriage in heaven; instead, this response was Jesus' refusal to answer the Sadducees' riddle and fall into their trap. Sidestepping their question about the much-married woman, he gave a definitive answer to their real question about the doctrine of resurrection. Because the Sadducees believed only in the Pentateuch (Genesis—Deuteronomy), Jesus quoted from Exodus 3:6 to prove that there is life after death. God spoke of Abraham, Isaac, and Jacob years after their deaths as if they *still lived*. God's covenant with all people exists beyond death.

12:26
†Exod 3:6
12:27
Matt 22:32
Luke 20:38

26"But now, as to whether the dead will be raised—haven't you ever read about this in the writings of Moses, in the story of the burning bush? Long after Abraham, Isaac, and Jacob had died, God said to Moses,* 'I am the God of Abraham, the God of Isaac, and the God of Jacob.'* 27So he is the God of the living, not the dead. You have made a serious error."

Religious Leaders Question Jesus about the Greatest Commandment
(**195**/Matthew 22:34-40)

12:29-30
†Deut 6:4-5
†Josh 22:5
Luke 10:27
12:31
†Lev 19:18
Rom 13:9
Gal 5:14
Jas 2:8
12:32
†Deut 4:35, 39; 6:4
1 Cor 8:4-6

28One of the teachers of religious law was standing there listening to the debate. He realized that Jesus had answered well, so he asked, "Of all the commandments, which is the most important?"

29Jesus replied, "The most important commandment is this: 'Listen, O Israel! The LORD our God is the one and only LORD. 30And you must love the LORD your God with all your heart, all your soul, all your mind, and all your strength.'* 31The second is equally important: 'Love your neighbor as yourself.'* No other commandment is greater than these."

32The teacher of religious law replied, "Well said, Teacher. You have spoken the truth by

12:26a Greek *in the story of the bush? God said to him.*   **12:26b** Exod 3:6.   **12:29-30** Deut 6:4-5.
12:31 Lev 19:18.

WHAT JESUS SAID ABOUT LOVE
In Mark 12:28 a teacher of religious law asked Jesus which of all the commandments was the most important to follow. Jesus mentioned two commandments, one from Deuteronomy 6:5, the other from Leviticus 19:18. Both had to do with love. Why is love so important? Jesus said that all of the comandments were given for two simple reasons: to help us love God and love others as we should.

What else did Jesus say about love?	Reference
God loves us	John 3:16
We are to love God	Matthew 22:37
Because God loves us, he cares for us	Matthew 6:25-34
God wants everyone to know how much he loves them.	John 17:23
God loves even those who hate him; we are to do the same	Matthew 5:43-47; Luke 6:35
God seeks out even those most alienated from him	Luke 15
God must be our first love	Matthew 6:24; 10:37
We love God when we obey him	John 14:21; 15:10
God loves Jesus, his Son.	John 5:20; 10:17
Jesus loves God.	John 14:31
Those who refuse Jesus don't have God's love	John 5:41-44
Jesus loves us just as God loves Jesus.	John 15:9
Jesus proved his love for us by dying on the cross so that we could live eternally with him	John 3:14, 15; 15:13, 14
The love between God and Jesus is the perfect example of how we are to love others	John 17:21-26
We are to love one another (John 13:34, 35) and demonstrate that love.	Matthew 5:40-42; 10:42
We are *not* to love the praise of people (John 12:43), selfish recognition (Matthew 23:6), earthly belongings (Luke 6:19-31), or anything more than God	Luke 16:13
Jesus' love extends to each individual	Mark 10:21; John 10:11-15
Jesus wants us to love him through the good and through the difficult times	Matthew 26:31-35
Jesus wants our love to be genuine.	John 21:15-17

• **12:28** By Jesus' time, the Jews had accumulated hundreds of laws—613 by one historian's count. Some religious leaders tried to distinguish between major and minor laws, and some taught that all laws were equally binding and that it was dangerous to make any distinctions. This teacher's question could have provoked controversy among these groups, but Jesus' answer summarized all of God's laws.

12:29-31 God's laws are not burdensome. They can be reduced to two simple principles: Love God and love others. These commands are from the Old Testament (Deuteronomy 6:5; Leviticus 19:18). When you love God completely and care for others as you care for yourself, then you have fulfilled the intent of the Ten Commandments and the other Old Testament laws. According to Jesus, these two commandments summarize all God's laws. Let

them rule your thoughts, decisions, and actions. When you are uncertain about what to do, ask yourself which course of action best demonstrates love for God and love for others.

12:32-34 This Pharisee had grasped the intent of God's law— that true obedience comes from the heart. Because all the Old Testament commands lead to Christ, his next step was faith in Jesus himself. This, however, was the most difficult step to take. We do not know if this Pharisee ever became a true believer, but we must remember that being "close" to being a Christian is infinitely far away if a person never commits to Christ. Salvation cannot rest on intellectual knowledge alone. You must repent, follow Christ, and be made a new person by his Holy Spirit. Don't be content with being close; take the step and make the commitment.

saying that there is only one God and no other. 33And I know it is important to love him with all my heart and all my understanding and all my strength, and to love my neighbor as myself. This is more important than to offer all of the burnt offerings and sacrifices required in the law."

34Realizing how much the man understood, Jesus said to him, "You are not far from the Kingdom of God." And after that, no one dared to ask him any more questions.

Religious Leaders Cannot Answer Jesus' Question
(**196**/Matthew 22:41-46; Luke 20:41-44)
35Later, as Jesus was teaching the people in the Temple, he asked, "Why do the teachers of religious law claim that the Messiah is the son of David? 36For David himself, speaking under the inspiration of the Holy Spirit, said,

'The LORD said to my Lord,
Sit in the place of honor at my right hand
    until I humble your enemies beneath your feet.'*

37Since David himself called the Messiah 'my Lord,' how can the Messiah be his son?" The large crowd listened to him with great delight.

Jesus Warns against the Religious Leaders (**197**/Matthew 23:1-12; Luke 20:45-47)
38Jesus also taught: "Beware of these teachers of religious law! For they like to parade around in flowing robes and receive respectful greetings as they walk in the marketplaces. 39And how they love the seats of honor in the synagogues and the head table at banquets. 40Yet they shamelessly cheat widows out of their property and then pretend to be pious by making long prayers in public. Because of this, they will be more severely punished."

A Poor Widow Gives All She Has (**200**/Luke 21:1-4)
41Jesus sat down near the collection box in the Temple and watched as the crowds dropped in their money. Many rich people put in large amounts. 42Then a poor widow came and dropped in two small coins.*

43Jesus called his disciples to him and said, "I tell you the truth, this poor widow has given more than all the others who are making contributions. 44For they gave a tiny part of their surplus, but she, poor as she is, has given everything she had to live on."

Jesus Tells about the Future (**201**/Matthew 24:1-25; Luke 21:5-24)

13 As Jesus was leaving the Temple that day, one of his disciples said, "Teacher, look at these magnificent buildings! Look at the impressive stones in the walls."

2Jesus replied, "Yes, look at these great buildings. But they will be completely demolished. Not one stone will be left on top of another!"

3Later, Jesus sat on the Mount of Olives across the valley from the Temple. Peter, James, John, and Andrew came to him privately and asked him, 4"Tell us, when will all this happen? What sign will show us that these things are about to be fulfilled?"

12:36 Ps 110:1.   **12:42** Greek *two lepta, which is a kodrantes* [i.e., a quadrans].

12:33
†Lev 19:18
Mic 6:6-8

12:34
Matt 22:46
Luke 20:40

12:36
2 Sam 23:2
†Ps 110:1

12:37
Rom 1:3; 9:5
Rev 22:16

12:39
Luke 11:43

12:41
2 Kgs 12:9
John 8:20

12:43-44
2 Cor 8:12

13:2
Luke 19:44

12:35-37 Jesus quoted Psalm 110:1 to show that David considered the Messiah to be his Lord, not just his descendant. The religious leaders did not understand that the Messiah would be far more than a human descendant of David; he would be God himself in human form.

● **12:38-40** Jesus again exposed the religious leaders' impure motives. The teachers received no pay, so they depended on the hospitality extended by devout Jews. Some of them used this custom to exploit people, cheating the poor out of everything they had and taking advantage of the rich. Through their pious actions they hoped to gain status, recognition, and respect.

● **12:38-40** Jesus warned against trying to make a good impression. These teachers of religious law were religious hypocrites who had no love for God. True followers of Christ are not distinguished by showy spirituality. Reading the Bible, praying in public, or following church rituals can be phony if the motive for doing them is to be noticed or honored. Let your actions be consistent with your beliefs. Live for Christ, even when no one is looking.

12:41 There were several boxes in the Temple where money could be placed. Some were for collecting the Temple tax from

Jewish males; the others were for freewill offerings. This particular collection box was probably in the Court of the Women.

12:41-44 This widow gave all she had to live on, in contrast to the way most people handle their money. When we consider giving a certain percentage of our income a great accomplishment, we resemble those who gave "a tiny part of their surplus." Here, Jesus was admiring generous and sacrificial giving. As believers, we should consider increasing our giving—whether of money, time, or talents—to a point beyond convenience or calculation.

13:1, 2 About 15 years before Jesus was born (20 B.C.), Herod the Great began to remodel and rebuild the Temple, which had stood for nearly 500 years since the days of Ezra (Ezra 6:14, 15). Herod made the Temple one of the most beautiful buildings in Jerusalem, not to honor God, but to appease the Jews whom he ruled. The magnificent building project was not completely finished until A.D. 64. Jesus' prophecy that not one stone would be left on another was fulfilled in A.D. 70, when the Romans completely destroyed the Temple and the entire city of Jerusalem.

● **13:3ff** The disciples wanted to know when the Temple would be destroyed. Jesus gave them a prophetic picture of that time,

13:5
2 Thes 2:3, 10-12
1 Tim 4:1
2 Tim 3:13
1 Jn 4:6

13:6
John 5:43

13:8
2 Chr 15:6
Isa 19:2

13:10
Rom 10:18

13:11
Matt 10:19-20
Luke 12:11-12

13:12
Mic 7:6

13:13
Matt 10:22
John 15:18-21

⁵Jesus replied, "Don't let anyone mislead you, ⁶for many will come in my name, claiming, 'I am the Messiah.'* They will deceive many. ⁷And you will hear of wars and threats of wars, but don't panic. Yes, these things must take place, but the end won't follow immediately. ⁸Nation will go to war against nation, and kingdom against kingdom. There will be earthquakes in many parts of the world, as well as famines. But this is only the first of the birth pains, with more to come.

⁹"When these things begin to happen, watch out! You will be handed over to the local councils and beaten in the synagogues. You will stand trial before governors and kings because you are my followers. But this will be your opportunity to tell them about me.* ¹⁰For the Good News must first be preached to all nations.* ¹¹But when you are arrested and stand trial, don't worry in advance about what to say. Just say what God tells you at that time, for it is not you who will be speaking, but the Holy Spirit.

¹²"A brother will betray his brother to death, a father will betray his own child, and children will rebel against their parents and cause them to be killed. ¹³And everyone will hate you because you are my followers.* But the one who endures to the end will be saved.

13:6 Greek *claiming, 'I am.'*   **13:9** Or *But this will be your testimony against them.*   **13:10** Or *all peoples.*
13:13 Greek *on account of my name.*

JESUS' PROPHECIES IN THE OLIVET DISCOURSE	Type of Prophecy	Old Testament References	Other New Testament References
	The Last Days		
	Mark 13:1-23	Daniel 9:26, 27	John 15:21
	Matthew 24:1-28	Daniel 11:31	Revelation 11:2
	Luke 21:5-24	Joel 2:2	1 Timothy 4:1, 2
	The Second Coming of Christ		
	Mark 13:24-27	Isaiah 13:6-10	Revelation 6:12
	Luke 21:25-28	Ezekiel 32:7	Mark 14:62
	Matthew 24:29-31	Daniel 7:13, 14	1 Thessalonians 4:16

In Mark 13, often called the Olivet discourse, Jesus talked a lot about two things: the end times and his second coming. Jesus was not trying to encourage his disciples to speculate about exactly when he would return by sharing these prophecies with them. Instead, he urges all his followers to be watchful and prepared for his coming. If we serve Jesus faithfully now, we will be ready when he returns.

---

including events leading up to it. He also talked about future events connected with his return to earth to judge all people. Jesus predicted both near and distant events without putting them in chronological order. Some of the disciples lived to see the destruction of Jerusalem in A.D. 70. This event would assure them that everything else Jesus predicted would also happen.

Jesus warned his followers about the future so that they could learn how to live in the present. Many predictions Jesus made in this passage have not yet been fulfilled. He did not make them so that we would guess when they might be fulfilled but to help us to be spiritually alert and prepared at all times as we wait for his return.

13:3, 4 The Mount of Olives rises above Jerusalem to the east. From its slopes a person can look down into the city and see the Temple. Zechariah 14:1-4 predicts that the Messiah will stand on this very mountain when he returns to set up his eternal Kingdom.

• **13:5-7** What are the signs of the end times? There have been people in every generation since Christ's resurrection claiming to know exactly when Jesus would return. No one has been right yet, however, because Christ will return on God's timetable, not ours. Jesus predicted that before his return, many believers would be misled by false teachers claiming to have revelations from God.

According to Scripture, one clear sign of Christ's return will be his unmistakable appearance in the clouds, which will be seen by all people (13:26; Revelation 1:7). In other words, you do not have to wonder whether a certain person is the Messiah or whether these are the "end times." When Jesus returns, *you will know* beyond a doubt, because it will be evident to all true

believers. Beware of groups who claim special knowledge of Christ's return because no one knows when that time will be (13:32). Be cautious about saying, "This is it!" but be bold in your total commitment to have your heart and life ready for Christ's return.

13:9-11 As the early church began to grow, most of the disciples experienced the kind of persecution Jesus was talking about. Since the time of Christ, Christians have been persecuted in their own lands and on foreign mission fields. Though you may be safe from persecution now, your vision of God's Kingdom must not be limited by what happens only to you. A glance at a newspaper will reveal that many Christians in other parts of the world daily face hardships and persecution. Persecutions are an opportunity for Christians to witness for Christ to those opposed to him. God's desire is that the Good News be proclaimed to everyone in spite of persecution.

13:11 Jesus was teaching the kind of attitude we should have when we must take a stand for the Good News. We don't have to be fearful or defensive about our faith because the Holy Spirit will be present to give us the right words to say.

• **13:13** To believe in Jesus and "endure to the end" will take perseverance because our faith will be challenged and opposed. Severe trials will sift true Christians from fair-weather believers. Enduring to the end does not earn salvation for us but marks us as already saved. The assurance of our salvation will keep us strong in times of persecution.

¹⁴"The day is coming when you will see the sacrilegious object that causes desecration* standing where he* should not be." (Reader, pay attention!) "Then those in Judea must flee to the hills. ¹⁵A person out on the deck of a roof must not go down into the house to pack. ¹⁶A person out in the field must not return even to get a coat. ¹⁷How terrible it will be for pregnant women and for nursing mothers in those days. ¹⁸And pray that your flight will not be in winter. ¹⁹For there will be greater anguish in those days than at any time since God created the world. And it will never be so great again. ²⁰In fact, unless the Lord shortens that time of calamity, not a single person will survive. But for the sake of his chosen ones he has shortened those days.

²¹"Then if anyone tells you, 'Look, here is the Messiah,' or 'There he is,' don't believe it. ²²For false messiahs and false prophets will rise up and perform signs and wonders so as to deceive, if possible, even God's chosen ones. ²³Watch out! I have warned you about this ahead of time!

Jesus Tells about His Return (**202**/Matthew 24:26-35; Luke 21:25-33)
²⁴"At that time, after the anguish of those days,

the sun will be darkened,
the moon will give no light,
²⁵ the stars will fall from the sky,
and the powers in the heavens will be shaken.*

²⁶Then everyone will see the Son of Man* coming on the clouds with great power and glory.* ²⁷And he will send out his angels to gather his chosen ones from all over the world*—from the farthest ends of the earth and heaven.

²⁸"Now learn a lesson from the fig tree. When its branches bud and its leaves begin to sprout, you know that summer is near. ²⁹In the same way, when you see all these things taking place, you can know that his return is very near, right at the door. ³⁰I tell you the truth, this generation* will not pass from the scene before all these things take place. ³¹Heaven and earth will disappear, but my words will never disappear.

Jesus Tells about Remaining Watchful (**203**/Matthew 24:36-51; Luke 21:34-38)
³²"However, no one knows the day or hour when these things will happen, not even the angels in heaven or the Son himself. Only the Father knows. ³³And since you don't know when that time will come, be on guard! Stay alert*!

13:14 | †Dan 9:27; 11:31; 12:11 / Matt 24:15 / 2 Thes 2:3
13:17 | Luke 23:29
13:19 | Dan 9:26; 12:1 / Joel 2:2 / Rev 7:14
13:21 | Luke 17:23
13:22 | Deut 13:1-3 / 2 Thes 2:9-10 / Rev 13:13
13:24-25 | †Isa 13:10; 34:4 / Ezek 32:7-8 / †Joel 2:10, 31; 3:15 / Rev 6:12-14; 8:12
13:26 | †Dan 7:13 / Matt 16:27 / Rev 1:7
13:27 | Deut 30:4 / Zech 2:6
13:31 | Matt 5:18 / Luke 16:17
13:32 | Acts 1:7
13:33-37 | Matt 25:13-14 / Luke 12:35-40 / Rom 13:11 / Eph 6:17-18 / Col 4:2 / 1 Thes 5:6

13:14a Greek *the abomination of desolation.* See Dan 9:27; 11:31; 12:11. **13:14b** Or *it.* **13:24-25** See Isa 13:10; 34:4; Joel 2:10. **13:26a** "Son of Man" is a title Jesus used for himself. **13:26b** See Dan 7:13. **13:27** Greek *from the four winds.* **13:30** Or *this age,* or *this nation.* **13:33** Some manuscripts add *and pray.*

13:14 The "sacrilegious object that causes desecration" refers to the desecration of the Temple by God's enemies. This happened repeatedly in Israel's history: in 597 B.C. when Nebuchadnezzar looted the Temple and took Judean captives to Babylon (2 Chronicles 36); in 168 B.C. when Antiochus Epiphanes sacrificed a pig to Zeus on the sacred Temple altar (Daniel 9:27; 11:30, 31); in A.D. 70 when the Roman general Titus placed an idol on the site of the burned-out Temple after the destruction of Jerusalem. Just a few years after Jesus gave this warning, in A.D. 38, the emperor Caligula made plans to put his own statue in the Temple, but he died before this could be carried out.

13:17 Some Christian couples who are contemplating pregnancy have been discouraged by this verse. They wonder if kids should be brought into a world filled with sin, evil, and terror. Jesus was not making a general warning against pregnancy, however. Many times in history have had risks and drawbacks; no place or time is perfect. We must remember that God will look out for the welfare of our children as he has looked out for us.

13:20 The "chosen ones" are God's chosen people, those who are saved. See Romans 8:29, 30 and Ephesians 1:4, 5 for more on God's choice.

13:22, 23 Is it possible for Christians to be deceived? Yes. So convincing will be the arguments and proofs from deceivers in the end times that it will be difficult *not* to fall away from Christ. If we are prepared, Jesus says, we can remain faithful. But if we are not prepared, we will turn away. To penetrate the disguises of false teachers we can ask: (1) Have their predictions come true, or do

they have to revise them to fit what's already happened? (2) Does any teaching utilize a small section of the Bible to the neglect of the whole? (3) Does the teaching contradict what the Bible says about God? (4) Are the practices meant to glorify the teacher or Christ? (5) Do the teachings promote hostility toward other Christians?

13:31 The truth that heaven and earth will disappear is all that much more believable in our age of nuclear power and terrorism. Jesus tells us, however, that even though the earth will pass away, the truth of his words will never be changed or abolished. God and his Word provide the only stability in our unstable world. How shortsighted people are who spend all their time and energy learning about this temporary world and accumulating its possessions, while neglecting the Bible and its eternal truths!

• **13:32** When Jesus said that even he did not know the time of the end, he was affirming his humanity. Of course God the Father knows the time, and Jesus and the Father are one. But when Jesus became a man, he voluntarily gave up the unlimited use of his divine attributes.

The emphasis of this verse is not on Jesus' lack of knowledge, but rather on the fact that no one knows. It is God the Father's secret to be revealed when he wills. No one can predict by Scripture or science the exact day of Jesus' return. Jesus is teaching that preparation, not calculation, is needed.

• **13:33, 34** Months of planning go into a wedding, the birth of a baby, a career change, a speaking engagement, the purchase of a home. Do you place the same importance on preparing for Christ's return, the most important event in your life? Its results

[34]"The coming of the Son of Man can be illustrated by the story of a man going on a long trip. When he left home, he gave each of his slaves instructions about the work they were to do, and he told the gatekeeper to watch for his return. [35]You, too, must keep watch! For you don't know when the master of the household will return—in the evening, at midnight, before dawn, or at daybreak. [36]Don't let him find you sleeping when he arrives without warning. [37]I say to you what I say to everyone: Watch for him!"

C. DEATH AND RESURRECTION OF JESUS, THE SERVANT (14:1—16:20)

Mark tells us about Jesus' ultimate deed of servanthood—dying for us on the cross. Jesus died for our sin so we wouldn't have to. Now we can have eternal fellowship with God instead of eternal suffering and death. When first written in Rome, this Gospel was encouraging to Roman Christians during times of persecution. Christ's victory through suffering can encourage us during difficult times, too.

Religious Leaders Plot to Kill Jesus (**207**/Matthew 26:1-5; Luke 22:1-2)

14:1-2
John 11:55-57

14 It was now two days before Passover and the Festival of Unleavened Bread. The leading priests and the teachers of religious law were still looking for an opportunity to capture Jesus secretly and kill him. [2]"But not during the Passover celebration," they agreed, "or the people may riot."

A Woman Anoints Jesus with Perfume (**182**/Matthew 26:6-13; John 12:1-11)

14:3
Luke 7:37-38

[3]Meanwhile, Jesus was in Bethany at the home of Simon, a man who had previously had leprosy. While he was eating,* a woman came in with a beautiful alabaster jar of expensive perfume made from essence of nard. She broke open the jar and poured the perfume over his head.

14:3 Or *reclining.*

---

will last for eternity. You dare not postpone your preparations because you do not know when his return will occur. The way to prepare is to study God's Word and live by its instructions each day. Only then will you be ready.

- **13:35-37** Mark 13 tells us how to live while we wait for Christ's return: (1) We are not to be misled by confusing claims or speculative interpretations of what will happen (13:5, 6). (2) We should not be afraid to tell people about Christ, despite what they might say or do to us (13:9-11). (3) We must stand firm by faith and not be surprised by persecution (13:13). (4) We must be morally alert, obedient to the commands for living found in God's Word. This chapter was not given to promote discussions on prophetic timetables but to stimulate right living for God in a world where he is largely ignored.

14:1 The Passover commemorated the night the Israelites were freed from Egypt (Exodus 12), when God "passed over" homes marked by the blood of a lamb while killing firstborn sons in unmarked homes. The day of Passover was followed by a seven-day festival called the Festival of Unleavened Bread. This, too, recalled the Israelites' quick escape from Egypt when they didn't have time to let their bread rise, so they baked it without yeast (leaven). On this holiday, Jewish families still gather for a special meal that includes lamb, wine, bitter herbs, and unleavened bread.

14:2 The Jews were preparing to observe Passover, a time of remembrance for families to celebrate when the blood of lambs had saved their ancestors. But some of the religious leaders had another agenda. Jesus had disrupted their security, revealed their sham, and opposed their authority. Now they would put him away. But the world is controlled by our all-wise God, not puny politicians. God would turn the religious leaders' murder plot into the greatest blessing that mankind would ever know. Another Lamb would be slain, and his blood would save all people. When grief or disaster seem to be dominating, remember that your life is in God's hands and remember what Jesus did for you.

14:3 Bethany is located on the eastern slope of the Mount of Olives (Jerusalem is on the western side). This town was the home of Jesus' friends Lazarus, Mary, and Martha, who were also present at this dinner (John 11:2). The woman who anointed Jesus' feet was Mary, Lazarus and Martha's sister (John 12:1-3).

14:3-9 Matthew and Mark placed this event just before the Last

Supper, while John placed it a week earlier, just before the Triumphal Entry. It must be remembered that the main purpose of the Gospel writers was not to present an exact chronological account of Christ's life but to give an accurate record of his message. Matthew and Mark may have chosen to place this event here to contrast the complete devotion of Mary with the betrayal of Judas, the next event in both Gospels.

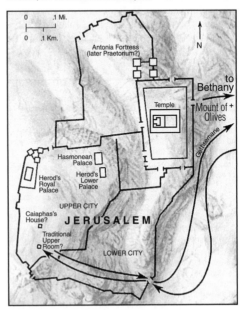

UPPER ROOM AND GETHSEMANE Jesus and the disciples ate the traditional Passover meal in an upper room in the city and then went to the Mount of Olives into a garden called Gethsemane. In the cool of the evening, Jesus prayed for strength to face the trial and suffering ahead.

⁴Some of those at the table were indignant. "Why waste such expensive perfume?" they asked. ⁵"It could have been sold for a year's wages* and the money given to the poor!" So they scolded her harshly.

⁶But Jesus replied, "Leave her alone. Why criticize her for doing such a good thing to me? ⁷You will always have the poor among you, and you can help them whenever you want to. But you will not always have me. ⁸She has done what she could and has anointed my body for burial ahead of time. ⁹I tell you the truth, wherever the Good News is preached throughout the world, this woman's deed will be remembered and discussed."

14:7
Deut 15:11
14:8
John 19:40

Judas Agrees to Betray Jesus (208/Matthew 26:14-16; Luke 22:3-6)

¹⁰Then Judas Iscariot, one of the twelve disciples, went to the leading priests to arrange to betray Jesus to them. ¹¹They were delighted when they heard why he had come, and they promised to give him money. So he began looking for an opportunity to betray Jesus.

Disciples Prepare for the Passover (209/Matthew 26:17-19; Luke 22:7-13)

¹²On the first day of the Festival of Unleavened Bread, when the Passover lamb is sacrificed, Jesus' disciples asked him, "Where do you want us to go to prepare the Passover meal for you?"

14:12
Exod 12:14-21
Deut 16:1-4
1 Cor 5:7-8

¹³So Jesus sent two of them into Jerusalem with these instructions: "As you go into the city, a man carrying a pitcher of water will meet you. Follow him. ¹⁴At the house he enters, say to the owner, 'The Teacher asks: Where is the guest room where I can eat the Passover meal with my disciples?' ¹⁵He will take you upstairs to a large room that is already set up. That is where you should prepare our meal." ¹⁶So the two disciples went into the city and found everything just as Jesus had said, and they prepared the Passover meal there.

14:14
Exod 12:8
Lev 23:5

Jesus and the Disciples Share the Last Supper
(211/Matthew 26:20-30; Luke 22:14-30; John 13:21-30)

¹⁷In the evening Jesus arrived with the twelve disciples.* ¹⁸As they were at the table* eating, Jesus said, "I tell you the truth, one of you eating with me here will betray me."

14:18
†Ps 41:9

¹⁹Greatly distressed, each one asked in turn, "Am I the one?"

²⁰He replied, "It is one of you twelve who is eating from this bowl with me. ²¹For the Son of Man* must die, as the Scriptures declared long ago. But how terrible it will be for the one who betrays him. It would be far better for that man if he had never been born!"

14:21
Ps 22:1-21
Isa 53:3-8

²²As they were eating, Jesus took some bread and blessed it. Then he broke it in pieces and gave it to the disciples, saying, "Take it, for this is my body."

14:22-25
1 Cor 11:23-25

²³And he took a cup of wine and gave thanks to God for it. He gave it to them, and they all

14:23
1 Cor 10:16

14:5 Greek *for 300 denarii*. A denarius was equivalent to a laborer's full day's wage.   **14:17** Greek *the Twelve*.
14:18 Or *As they reclined*.   **14:21** "Son of Man" is a title Jesus used for himself.

• **14:4, 5** Where Mark says "some of those at the table," John specifically mentions Judas (John 12:4, 5). Judas's indignation over Mary's act of worship was based not on concern for the poor but on greed. Because Judas was the treasurer of Jesus' ministry and had embezzled funds (John 12:6), he no doubt wanted the perfume sold so that he could benefit from the proceeds.

14:6, 7 Jesus was not saying that we should neglect the poor, nor was he justifying indifference to them. (For Jesus' teaching about the poor, see Matthew 6:2-4; Luke 6:20, 21; 14:13, 21; 18:22.) Jesus was praising Mary for her unselfish act of worship. The essence of worshiping Christ is to regard him with utmost love, respect, and devotion and to be willing to sacrifice to him what is most precious.

• **14:10** Why would Judas want to betray Jesus? Very likely, Judas expected Jesus to start a political rebellion and overthrow Rome. As treasurer, Judas certainly assumed (as did the other disciples, see 10:35-37) that he would be given an important position in Jesus' new government. But when Jesus praised Mary for pouring out the perfume, thought to be worth a day's salary, Judas finally began to realize that Jesus' Kingdom was not physical or political. Judas's greedy desire for money and status could not be fulfilled if he followed Jesus, so he betrayed him in exchange for money and favor from the religious leaders.

14:13 The two men Jesus sent were Peter and John (Luke 22:8).

14:14, 15 Many homes had large upstairs rooms, sometimes with stairways both inside and outside the house. The preparations for the Passover would have included setting the table and buying and preparing the Passover lamb, unleavened bread, sauces, and other ceremonial food and drink.

14:19 Judas, the very man who would betray Jesus, was at the table with the others. Judas had already determined to betray Jesus, but in cold-blooded hypocrisy he shared the fellowship of this meal. It is easy to become enraged or shocked by what Judas did; yet professing commitment to Christ and then denying him with one's life is also betraying him. It is denying Christ's love to disobey him; it is denying his truth to distrust him; it is denying his deity to reject his authority. Do your words and actions match?

14:20 It was often the practice to eat from a common bowl. Meat or bread was dipped into a bowl filled with sauce often made from fruit.

14:22-25 Mark records the origin of the Last Supper, which is still celebrated in worship services today. Jesus and his disciples ate a meal, sang psalms, read Scripture, and prayed. Then Jesus took two traditional parts of the Passover meal, the passing of bread and the drinking of wine, and gave them new meaning as representations of his body and blood. He used the bread and wine to explain the significance of what he was about to do on the cross. For more on the significance of the Last Supper, see 1 Corinthians 11:23-29.

The Last Supper is remembered by different terms. Each name

JUDAS ISCARIOT

It is easy to overlook the fact that Jesus chose Judas to be his disciple. We may also forget that while Judas betrayed Jesus, *all* the disciples abandoned him. With the other disciples, Judas shared a persistent misunderstanding of Jesus' mission. They all expected Jesus to make the right political moves. When he kept talking about dying, they all felt varying degrees of anger, fear, and disappointment. They didn't understand why they had been chosen if Jesus' mission was doomed to fail.

The exact motivation behind Judas's betrayal is unknown. What is clear is that Judas allowed his desires to place him in a position where Satan could manipulate him. Judas accepted payment to set Jesus up for the religious leaders. He identified Jesus for the guards in the dimly lit Garden of Gethsemane. It is possible that he was trying to force Jesus' hand: Would Jesus now rebel against Rome and set up a new political government?

Whatever his plan, though, at some point Judas realized he didn't like the way things were turning out. He tried to undo the evil he had done by returning the money to the priests, but it was too late. The wheels of God's sovereign plan had been set into motion. How sad that Judas ended his life in despair without ever experiencing the gift of reconciliation God could give even to him through Jesus Christ.

Human feelings toward Judas have always been mixed. Some have fervently hated him for his betrayal. Others have pitied him for not realizing what he was doing. A few have tried to make him a hero for his part in ending Jesus' earthly mission. Some have questioned God's fairness in allowing one man to bear such guilt. While there are many feelings about Judas, there are some facts to consider as well. He, by his own choice, betrayed God's Son into the hands of soldiers (Luke 22:48). He was a thief (John 12:6). Jesus knew that Judas's life of evil would not change (John 6:70). Judas's betrayal of Jesus was part of God's sovereign plan (Psalm 41:9; Zechariah 11:12-13; Matthew 20:18; 26:20-25; Acts 1:16, 20).

In betraying Jesus, Judas made the greatest mistake in history. But the fact that Jesus knew Judas would betray him doesn't mean that Judas was a puppet of God's will. Judas made the choice. God knew what that choice would be and confirmed it. Judas didn't lose his relationship with Jesus; rather, he never found Jesus in the first place. He is called "the one headed for destruction" (John 17:12) because he was never saved.

Judas does us a favor if he makes us think a second time about our commitment to God and the presence of God's Spirit within us. Are we true disciples and followers, or uncommitted pretenders? We can choose despair and death, or we can choose repentance, forgiveness, hope, and eternal life. Judas's betrayal sent Jesus to the cross to guarantee that second choice, our only chance. Will we accept Jesus' free gift, or, like Judas, betray him?

Strengths and accomplishments	• He was chosen as one of the 12 disciples; the only non-Galilean • He was in charge of the disciples' funds • He was able to recognize the evil in his betrayal of Jesus
Weaknesses and mistakes	• He was greedy (John 12:6) • He betrayed Jesus • He committed suicide instead of seeking forgiveness
Lessons from his life	• Evil plans and motives leave us open to being used by Satan for even greater evil • The consequences of evil are so devastating that even small lies and little wrongdoings have serious results • God's plan and his purposes are worked out even in the worst possible events
Vital statistics	• Where: Possibly from the town of Kerioth • Occupation: Disciple of Jesus • Relative: Father: Simon • Contemporaries: Jesus, Pilate, Herod, the other 11 disciples
Key verses	"Then Satan entered into Judas Iscariot, who was one of the twelve disciples, and he went to the leading priests and captains of the Temple guard to discuss the best way to betray Jesus to them" (Luke 22:3-4).

Judas's story is told in the Gospels. He is also mentioned in Acts 1:18-19.

---

believers use for this sacrament brings out a different dimension to it. It is the "Lord's Supper" because it commemorates the Passover meal that Jesus ate with his disciples; it is the "Eucharist" (thanksgiving) because in it we thank God for Christ's work for us; it is "Communion" because through it we commune with God and with other believers. As we eat the bread and drink the wine, we should be quietly reflective as we recall Jesus' death and his promise to come again, grateful for God's wonderful gift to us, and joyful as we meet with Christ and the body of believers.

14:23 Whatever name your church uses for this event (Communion, Lord's Supper, or Eucharist) and on whatever

schedule you celebrate it, the importance is that through celebrating Communion together believers experience the presence of Christ. The celebration of Communion: (1) humbles us before God. We confess our sin and restate our need for Christ to guide us. (2) reminds us that we are forgiven. We remember that his shed blood paid the price. (3) expresses our oneness in Christ. We are unified in our faith. (4) encourages us to recommit. We are reminded to pledge ourselves to serve him who died for us.

drank from it. 24And he said to them, "This is my blood, which confirms the covenant* between God and his people. It is poured out as a sacrifice for many. 25I tell you the truth, I will not drink wine again until the day I drink it new in the Kingdom of God."

26Then they sang a hymn and went out to the Mount of Olives.

Jesus Again Predicts Peter's Denial (222/Matthew 26:31-35)

27On the way, Jesus told them, "All of you will desert me. For the Scriptures say,

> 'God will strike* the Shepherd,
>   and the sheep will be scattered.'

14:27
†Zech 13:7

28But after I am raised from the dead, I will go ahead of you to Galilee and meet you there."

14:28
Mark 16:7

29Peter said to him, "Even if everyone else deserts you, I never will."

30Jesus replied, "I tell you the truth, Peter—this very night, before the rooster crows twice, you will deny three times that you even know me."

31"No!" Peter declared emphatically. "Even if I have to die with you, I will never deny you!" And all the others vowed the same.

Jesus Agonizes in the Garden (223/Matthew 26:36-46; Luke 22:39-46)

32They went to the olive grove called Gethsemane, and Jesus said, "Sit here while I go and pray." 33He took Peter, James, and John with him, and he became deeply troubled and distressed. 34He told them, "My soul is crushed with grief to the point of death. Stay here and keep watch with me."

14:33
Matt 17:1
Mark 9:2
Luke 9:28

14:34
†Pss 42:6; 43:5
John 12:27

35He went on a little farther and fell to the ground. He prayed that, if it were possible, the awful hour awaiting him might pass him by. 36"Abba, Father," * he cried out, "everything is possible for you. Please take this cup of suffering away from me. Yet I want your will to be done, not mine."

14:36
Matt 20:22
John 5:30; 6:38;
18:11
Rom 8:15
Gal 4:6

37Then he returned and found the disciples asleep. He said to Peter, "Simon, are you asleep? Couldn't you watch with me even one hour? 38Keep watch and pray, so that you will not give in to temptation. For the spirit is willing, but the body is weak."

14:38
Rom 7:22-23

39Then Jesus left them again and prayed the same prayer as before. 40When he returned to them again, he found them sleeping, for they couldn't keep their eyes open. And they didn't know what to say.

41When he returned to them the third time, he said, "Go ahead and sleep. Have your rest. But no—the time has come. The Son of Man is betrayed into the hands of sinners. 42Up, let's be going. Look, my betrayer is here!"

14:24 Some manuscripts read *the new covenant.*   **14:27** Greek *I will strike.* Zech 13:7.   **14:36** *Abba* is an Aramaic term for "father."

14:24 Jesus' death for us on the cross seals a new covenant between God and us. The old covenant involved forgiveness of sins through the blood of an animal sacrifice (Exodus 24:6-8). But instead of a spotless lamb on the altar, Jesus offered himself, the spotless Lamb of God, as a sacrifice that would forgive sin once and for all. Jesus was the final sacrifice for sins, and his blood sealed the new covenant between God and us. Now all of us can come to God through Jesus, in full confidence that God will hear us and save us from our sins.

14:26 The hymn they sang was most likely taken from Psalms 115–118, traditionally sung at the Passover meal.

• **14:27-31** This was the second time in the same evening that Jesus predicted the disciples' denial and desertion, which probably explains their strong reaction (14:31). For Jesus' earlier prediction, see Luke 22:31-34 and John 13:36-38.

14:31 Peter was so emphatic. It is easy to say we are devoted to Christ, but our claims are meaningful only when they are tested in the crucible of persecution. How strong is your faith? Is it strong enough to stand up under intense trial? We need the Holy Spirit, not boastfulness and human resolve. We must never discount our vulnerability to pride, greed, or even indifference.

14:35, 36 Was Jesus trying to get out of his task? Jesus expressed his true feelings, but he did not deny or rebel against God's will. He reaffirmed his desire to do what God wanted. Jesus' prayer highlights the terrible suffering he had to endure—an agony so much more magnified because he had to take on the sins of the whole world. This "cup" was the agony of alienation from God, his Father, at the cross (Hebrews 5:7-9). The sinless Son of God took on our sins and was separated for a while from God so that we could be eternally saved.

14:36 While praying, Jesus was aware of what doing the Father's will would cost him. He understood the suffering he was about to encounter, and he did not want to have to endure the horrible experience. But Jesus prayed, "Yet I want your will to be done, not mine." Anything worth having costs something. What does your commitment to God cost you? We must be willing to pay any price to gain what is priceless—eternal life.

14:38 You may not face execution for your faith, but you probably face many problems that wear you down. You deal with irritating people whom you must love and serve; you face the burden of unfinished tasks or lack of obvious results; you cope with helpers who let you down or fail to comprehend. Remember that in times of great stress, you are vulnerable to temptation, even if you have a willing spirit. Jesus explained how to resist: (1) *Keep watch* (14:34)—stay awake and be morally vigilant. (2) *Pray to God* (14:35)—this is how you maintain your vigilance. (3) *Seek support of friends and loved ones* (14:33, 37, 40, 41)—this is how you build up your resistance and help others; when one is weak, others are strong. (4) *Focus on the purpose God has given you* (14:36)—this is how you do God's will and not your own.

Jesus Is Betrayed and Arrested
(**224**/Matthew 26:47-56; Luke 22:47-53; John 18:1-11)
43And immediately, even as Jesus said this, Judas, one of the twelve disciples, arrived with a crowd of men armed with swords and clubs. They had been sent by the leading priests, the teachers of religious law, and the elders. 44The traitor, Judas, had given them a prearranged signal: "You will know which one to arrest when I greet him with a kiss. Then you can take him away under guard." 45As soon as they arrived, Judas walked up to Jesus. "Rabbi!" he exclaimed, and gave him the kiss.

14:47
John 18:10

46Then the others grabbed Jesus and arrested him. 47But one of the men with Jesus pulled out his sword and struck the high priest's slave, slashing off his ear.

14:49
Isa 53:7-9
Luke 24:44

48Jesus asked them, "Am I some dangerous revolutionary, that you come with swords and clubs to arrest me? 49Why didn't you arrest me in the Temple? I was there among you teaching every day. But these things are happening to fulfill what the Scriptures say about me."

14:50
Ps 88:8
John 16:32

50Then all his disciples deserted him and ran away. 51One young man following behind was clothed only in a long linen shirt. When the mob tried to grab him, 52he slipped out of his shirt and ran away naked.

MAJOR EVENTS OF PASSION WEEK	Day	Event	References
Sunday through Wednesday Jesus spent each night in Bethany, just two miles east of Jerusalem on the opposite slope of the Mount of Olives. He probably stayed at the home of Mary, Martha, and Lazarus. Jesus spent Thursday night praying in the Garden of Gethsemane. Friday and Saturday nights Jesus' body lay in the garden tomb.	Sunday	Triumphal Entry into Jerusalem	Matthew 21:1-11; Mark 11:1-10; Luke 19:29-40; John 12:12-19
	Monday	Jesus clears the Temple	Matthew 21:12, 13; Mark 11:15-17; Luke 19:45, 46
	Tuesday	Jesus' authority challenged in the Temple	Matthew 21:23-27; Mark 11:27-33; Luke 20:1-8
		Jesus teaches in stories and confronts the Jewish leaders	Matthew 21:28–23:36; Mark 12:1-40; Luke 20:9-47
		Greeks ask to see Jesus	John 12:20-26
		The Olivet discourse	Matthew 24; Mark 13; Luke 21:5-38
		Judas agrees to betray Jesus	Matthew 26:14-16; Mark 14:10, 11; Luke 22:3-6
	Wednesday	The Bible does not say what Jesus did on this day; he probably remained in Bethany with his disciples	
	Thursday	The Last Supper	Matthew 26:26-29; Mark 14:22-25; Luke 22:14-20
		Jesus speaks to the disciples in the upper room	John 13–17
		Jesus struggles in Gethsemane	Matthew 26:36-46; Mark 14:32-42; Luke 22:39-46; John 18:1
		Jesus is betrayed and arrested	Matthew 26:47-56; Mark 14:43-52; Luke 22:47-53; John 18:2-12
	Friday	Jesus is tried by Jewish and Roman authorities and is denied by Peter	Matthew 26:57–27:2, 11-31; Mark 14:53–15:20; Luke 22:54–23:25; John 18:13–19:16
		Jesus is crucified	Matthew 27:31-56; Mark 15:20-41; Luke 23:26-49; John 19:17-30
	Sunday	The Resurrection	Matthew 28:1-10; Mark 16:1-11; Luke 24:1-12; John 20:1-18

14:43-45 Judas was given a contingent of police and soldiers (John 18:3) in order to seize Jesus and bring him before the religious court for trial. The religious leaders had issued a warrant for Jesus' arrest, and Judas was acting as Jesus' official accuser.

14:47 According to John 18:10, the person who pulled out a sword was Peter. Luke 22:51 records that Jesus healed the man's ear and prevented any further bloodshed.

• **14:50** Just hours earlier, these disciples had vowed never to desert Jesus (14:31).

14:51, 52 Tradition says that this young man may have been John Mark, the writer of this Gospel. The incident is not mentioned in any of the other accounts.

Caiaphas Questions Jesus (**226**/Matthew 26:57-68)

53They took Jesus to the high priest's home where the leading priests, the elders, and the teachers of religious law had gathered. 54Meanwhile, Peter followed him at a distance and went right into the high priest's courtyard. There he sat with the guards, warming himself by the fire.

55Inside, the leading priests and the entire high council* were trying to find evidence against Jesus, so they could put him to death. But they couldn't find any. 56Many false witnesses spoke against him, but they contradicted each other. 57Finally, some men stood up and gave this false testimony: 58"We heard him say, 'I will destroy this Temple made with human hands, and in three days I will build another, made without human hands.'" 59But even then they didn't get their stories straight!

60Then the high priest stood up before the others and asked Jesus, "Well, aren't you going to answer these charges? What do you have to say for yourself?" 61But Jesus was silent and made no reply. Then the high priest asked him, "Are you the Messiah, the Son of the Blessed One?"

62Jesus said, "I AM.* And you will see the Son of Man seated in the place of power at God's right hand* and coming on the clouds of heaven.*"

63Then the high priest tore his clothing to show his horror and said, "Why do we need other witnesses? 64You have all heard his blasphemy. What is your verdict?"

"Guilty!" they all cried. "He deserves to die!"

65Then some of them began to spit at him, and they blindfolded him and beat him with their fists. "Prophesy to us," they jeered. And the guards slapped him as they took him away.

14:54
Matt 26:3
John 18:18

14:56
Ps 35:11
Prov 6:16-19;
19:5

14:58
Mark 15:29
John 2:19

14:61
Isa 53:7
1 Pet 2:23

14:62
†Ps 110:1
†Dan 7:13
Matt 16:27; 24:30
Mark 8:38; 13:26
Acts 1:11
1 Thes 4:16
2 Thes 1:7
Rev 1:7; 22:20

14:63
Lev 10:6; 21:10
Num 14:6

14:64
Lev 24:16
John 19:7

14:65
Isa 50:6; 53:5

Peter Denies Knowing Jesus
(**227**/Matthew 26:69-75; Luke 22:54-65; John 18:25-27)

66Meanwhile, Peter was in the courtyard below. One of the servant girls who worked for the high priest came by 67and noticed Peter warming himself at the fire. She looked at him closely and said, "You were one of those with Jesus of Nazareth.*"

14:55 Greek *the Sanhedrin*. **14:62a** Or *The 'I AM' is here*; or *I am the LORD*. See Exod 3:14. **14:62b** Greek *at the right hand of the power*. See Ps 110:1. **14:62c** See Dan 7:13. **14:67** Or *Jesus the Nazarene*.

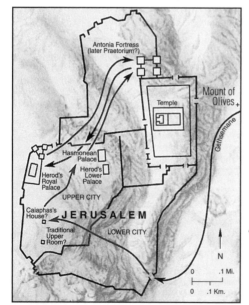

JESUS' TRIAL From Gethsemane, Jesus' trial began at the home of Caiaphas, the high priest. Jesus was then taken to Pilate, the Roman governor. Luke records that Pilate sent him to Herod, who was in Jerusalem—presumably in one of his two palaces (Luke 23:5-12). Herod sent him back to Pilate, who handed Jesus over to be crucified.

14:53ff This trial by the high council had two phases. A small group met at night (John 18:12-24), and then the full high council met at daybreak (Luke 22:66-71). They tried Jesus for religious offenses, such as calling himself the Son of God, which, according to law, was blasphemy. The trial was fixed: These religious leaders had already decided to kill Jesus (Luke 22:2).

14:55 The Romans controlled Israel, but the Jews were given some authority over religious and minor civil disputes. The Jewish ruling body, the high council, was made up of 71 of Israel's religious leaders. It was assumed that these men would be just. Instead, they showed great injustice in the trial of Jesus, even to the point of making up lies to use against him (14:57).

14:58 The statement that the false witnesses finally agreed to use as an accusation twisted Jesus' actual words. Jesus did not say, "I will destroy this Temple made with human hands"; he said, "Destroy this temple, and in three days I will raise it up" (John 2:19). Jesus was not talking about Herod's Temple but about his own body.

• **14:60-64** To the first question, Jesus made no reply because it was based on confusing and erroneous evidence. Not answering was wiser than trying to clarify the fabricated accusations. But if Jesus had refused to answer the second question, it could have been taken as a denial of his mission. Instead, his answer predicted a powerful role reversal. Sitting at God's right hand in the place of power, he would come to judge his accusers, and they would have to answer *his* questions (Psalm 110:1; Revelation 20:11-13).

14:66, 67 Caiaphas's home, where Jesus was tried (14:53), was part of a huge palace with several courtyards. John was apparently acquainted with the high priest, and he was let into the courtyard along with Peter (John 18:15, 16).

68But Peter denied it. "I don't know what you're talking about," he said, and he went out into the entryway. Just then, a rooster crowed.*

69When the servant girl saw him standing there, she began telling the others, "This man

14:70
Acts 2:7

is definitely one of them!" 70But Peter denied it again.

A little later some of the other bystanders confronted Peter and said, "You must be one of them, because you are a Galilean."

71Peter swore, "A curse on me if I'm lying—I don't know this man you're talking about!"

14:72
Mark 14:30

72And immediately the rooster crowed the second time.

Suddenly, Jesus' words flashed through Peter's mind: "Before the rooster crows twice, you will deny three times that you even know me." And he broke down and wept.

The Council of Religious Leaders Condemns Jesus
(228/Matthew 27:1-2; Luke 22:66-71)

15:1
Matt 27:1
Luke 23:1
John 18:28

15 Very early in the morning the leading priests, the elders, and the teachers of religious law—the entire high council*—met to discuss their next step. They bound Jesus, led him away, and took him to Pilate, the Roman governor.

Jesus Stands Trial before Pilate
(230/Matthew 27:11-14; Luke 23:1-5; John 18:28-37)

2Pilate asked Jesus, "Are you the king of the Jews?"

Jesus replied, "You have said it."

3Then the leading priests kept accusing him of many crimes, 4and Pilate asked him,

15:5
Isa 53:7
Mark 14:60-61
Luke 23:9

"Aren't you going to answer them? What about all these charges they are bringing against you?" 5But Jesus said nothing, much to Pilate's surprise.

14:68 Some manuscripts do not include *Just then, a rooster crowed.*   **15:1** Greek *the Sanhedrin;* also in 15:43.

WHY DID JESUS HAVE TO DIE?		
WHY DID JESUS HAVE TO DIE?	The Problem	We have all done things that are wrong, and we have failed to obey God's laws. Because of this, we have been separated from God our Creator. Separation from God is death; but, by ourselves, we can do nothing to become united with God.
	Why Jesus Could Help	Jesus was not only a man; he was God's unique Son. Because Jesus never disobeyed God and never sinned, only he can bridge the gap between the sinless God and sinful people.
	The Solution	Jesus freely offered his life for us, dying on the cross in our place, taking all our wrongdoing upon himself, and saving us from the consequences of sin—including God's judgment and death.
	The Results	Jesus took our past, present, and future sins upon himself so that we could have new life. Because all our wrongdoing is forgiven, we are reconciled to God. Furthermore, Jesus' resurrection from the dead is the proof that his substitutionary sacrifice on the cross was acceptable to God, and his resurrection has become the source of new life for those who believe that Jesus is the Son of God. All who believe in him may have this new life and live it in union with him.

• **14:71** It is easy to get angry at the high council and the Roman governor for their injustice in condemning Jesus, but Peter and the rest of the disciples also contributed to Jesus' pain by deserting him (14:50). While most of us may not be like the Jewish and Roman leaders, we are like the disciples because all of us have been guilty of denying Christ as Lord in vital areas of our lives. We may pride ourselves that we have not committed certain sins, but we are all guilty of sin. Don't try to excuse yourself by pointing at others whose sins seem worse than yours.

• **15:1** Why did the Jewish leaders send Jesus to Pilate, the Roman governor? The Romans had taken away the Jews' right to inflict capital punishment; so in order for Jesus to be condemned to death, he had to be sentenced by a Roman leader. The Jewish leaders wanted Jesus executed on a cross, a method of death that they believed brought a curse from God (see Deuteronomy 21:23). They hoped to persuade the people that Jesus was cursed, not blessed, by God.

15:3, 4 The Jewish leaders had to fabricate new accusations against Jesus when they brought him before Pilate. The charge of blasphemy would mean nothing to the Roman governor, so they accused Jesus of three other crimes: (1) encouraging the people to not pay their taxes to Rome, (2) claiming he was a king—"the King of the Jews," and (3) causing riots all over the countryside. Tax evasion, treason, and terrorism—all these would be cause for Pilate's concern (see also Luke 23:2).

15:5 Why didn't Jesus answer Pilate's questions? It would have been futile to answer, and the time had come to give his life to save the world. Jesus had no reason to try to prolong the trial or save himself. His was the ultimate example of self-assurance and peace, which no ordinary criminal could imitate. Nothing would stop him from completing the work he had come to earth to do (Isaiah 53:7).

Pilate Hands Jesus Over to Be Crucified
(**232**/Matthew 27:15-26; Luke 23:13-25; John 18:38–19:16)
⁶Now it was the governor's custom each year during the Passover celebration to release one prisoner—anyone the people requested. ⁷One of the prisoners at that time was Barabbas, a revolutionary who had committed murder in an uprising. ⁸The crowd went to Pilate and asked him to release a prisoner as usual.

⁹"Would you like me to release to you this 'King of the Jews'?" Pilate asked. ¹⁰(For he realized by now that the leading priests had arrested Jesus out of envy.) ¹¹But at this point the leading priests stirred up the crowd to demand the release of Barabbas instead of Jesus. ¹²Pilate asked them, "Then what should I do with this man you call the king of the Jews?"

¹³They shouted back, "Crucify him!"

¹⁴"Why?" Pilate demanded. "What crime has he committed?"

But the mob roared even louder, "Crucify him!"

¹⁵So to pacify the crowd, Pilate released Barabbas to them. He ordered Jesus flogged with a lead-tipped whip, then turned him over to the Roman soldiers to be crucified.

15:11
Acts 3:14

15:15
Isa 53:6

Roman Soldiers Mock Jesus (**233**/Matthew 27:27-31)
¹⁶The soldiers took Jesus into the courtyard of the governor's headquarters (called the Praetorium) and called out the entire regiment. ¹⁷They dressed him in a purple robe, and they wove thorn branches into a crown and put it on his head. ¹⁸Then they saluted him and taunted, "Hail! King of the Jews!" ¹⁹And they struck him on the head with a reed stick, spit on him, and dropped to their knees in mock worship. ²⁰When they were finally tired of mocking him, they took off the purple robe and put his own clothes on him again. Then they led him away to be crucified.

15:7 Barabbas was arrested for his part in a rebellion against the Roman government, and, although he had committed a murder, he may have been a hero among the Jews. The fiercely independent Jews hated to be ruled by pagan Romans. They hated paying taxes to support the despised government and its gods. Most of the Roman authorities who had to settle Jewish disputes hated the Jews in return. The time was ripe for rebellion.

15:8 This crowd was most likely a group of people loyal to the Jewish leaders. But where were the disciples and the crowds who days earlier had shouted, "Praise God in highest heaven"

(11:10)? Jesus' sympathizers were afraid of the Jewish leaders, so they went into hiding. Another possibility is that the multitude included many people who were in the Palm Sunday parade but who turned against Jesus when they saw that he was not going to be an earthly conqueror and their deliverer from Rome.

15:10 The Jewish leaders hated Pilate, but they went to him for the favor of condemning Jesus to crucifixion. Pilate could see that this was a frame-up. Why else would these people, who hated him and the Roman Empire he represented, ask him to convict one of their fellow Jews of treason and give him the death penalty?

• **15:13** Crucifixion was the Roman penalty for rebellion. Only slaves or those who were not Roman citizens could be crucified. If Jesus died by crucifixion, he would die the death of a rebel and slave, not of the king he claimed to be. This is just what the Jewish religious leaders wanted and the reason they whipped the mob into a frenzy. In addition, crucifixion would put the responsibility for killing Jesus on the Romans.

• **15:15** The region of Judea where Pilate ruled as governor was little more than a hot and dusty outpost of the Roman Empire. Because Judea was so far from Rome, Pilate was given just a small army. His primary job was to keep the peace. We know from historical records that Pilate had already been warned about other uprisings in his region. Although he may have seen no guilt in Jesus and no reason to condemn him to death, Pilate wavered when the Jews in the crowd threatened to report him to Caesar (John 19:12). Such a report, accompanied by a riot, could cost him his position and hopes for advancement.

Although Jesus was innocent according to Roman law, Pilate caved in to political pressure. He abandoned what he knew was right. Trying to second-guess the Jewish leaders, Pilate gave a decision that would please everyone while keeping himself safe. When we ignore God's clear statements of right and wrong and make decisions based on the preferences of our audience, we fall into compromise and lawlessness. God promises to honor those who do right, not those who make everyone happy.

15:19 The brutal guards, the power-hungry governor, and the conniving religious leaders had the upper hand. But they did not know the true power and authority of this man they were torturing and had condemned to death. Worldly powers and philosophies that mock Jesus' lordship will not be so arrogant when Jesus

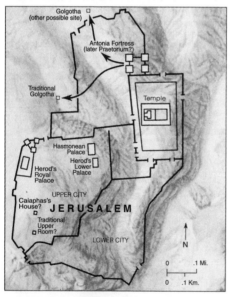

JESUS' ROUTE TO GOLGOTHA After being sentenced by Pilate, Jesus was taken from the praetorium to Golgotha, a place outside the city, for crucifixion.

Jesus Is Led Away to Be Crucified
(234/Matthew 27:32-34; Luke 23:26-31; John 19:17)

15:23
Ps 69:21

²¹A passerby named Simon, who was from Cyrene,* was coming in from the countryside just then, and the soldiers forced him to carry Jesus' cross. (Simon was the father of Alexander and Rufus.) ²²And they brought Jesus to a place called Golgotha (which means "Place of the Skull"). ²³They offered him wine drugged with myrrh, but he refused it.

Jesus Is Placed on the Cross
(235/Matthew 27:35-44; Luke 23:32-43; John 19:18-27)

15:24
†Ps 22:18

15:25
John 19:14

²⁴Then the soldiers nailed him to the cross. They divided his clothes and threw dice* to decide who would get each piece. ²⁵It was nine o'clock in the morning when they crucified

15:21 *Cyrene* was a city in northern Africa.   **15:24** Greek *cast lots.* See Ps 22:18.

PILATE

In Jesus' day, any death sentence had to be approved by the Roman official in charge of the administrative district. Pontius Pilate was governor of the province of Judea, where Jerusalem was located. When the Jewish leaders had Jesus in their power and wanted to kill him, they had to obtain Pilate's permission. So it happened that early one morning Pilate found a crowd at his door demanding a man's death.

Pilate's relationship with the Jews had always been stormy. His Roman toughness and fairness had been weakened by cynicism, compromises, and mistakes. On several occasions his actions had deeply offended the religious leaders. The resulting riots and chaos must have made Pilate wonder what he had gotten himself into. He was trying to control people who treated their Roman conquerors without respect. Jesus' trial was another episode in Pilate's ongoing problems.

For Pilate, there was never a doubt about Jesus' innocence. Three separate times he declared Jesus not guilty. He couldn't understand why these people wanted to kill Jesus, but his fear of the Jews' political pressure made him decide to allow Jesus' crucifixion. Because of the people's threat to inform the emperor that Pilate hadn't eliminated a rebel against Rome, Pilate went against what he knew was right. In desperation, he chose to do wrong.

We share a common humanity with Pilate. At times we know what is right but choose what is wrong. He had his moment in history, and now we have ours. What have we done with our opportunities and responsibilities? What judgment have we passed on Jesus?

Strength and accomplishment	• Roman governor of Judea
Weaknesses and mistakes	• He failed in his attempt to rule a people who were defeated militarily but never dominated by Rome • His constant political struggles made him a cynical and uncaring compromiser, susceptible to pressure • Although he realized Jesus was innocent, he bowed to the public demand for his execution
Lessons from his life	• Great evil can happen when truth is at the mercy of political pressures • Resisting the truth leaves a person without purpose or direction
Vital statistics	• Where: Judea • Occupation: Roman governor of Judea • Relative: Wife: unnamed • Contemporaries: Jesus, Caiaphas, Herod
Key verses	"'What is truth?' Pilate asked. Then he went out again to the people and told them, 'He is not guilty of any crime. But you have a custom of asking me to release one prisoner each year at Passover. Would you like me to release this "King of the Jews"?'" (John 18:38-39).

Pilate's story is told in the Gospels. He is also mentioned in Acts 3:13; 4:27; 13:28; 1 Timothy 6:13.

---

returns in judgment (see Philippians 2:10, 11). When you feel that unjust people who have control and viewpoints hostile to Christianity are carrying the day, rest assured that Jesus holds the highest place and will return in glory.

15:21 Colonies of Jews existed outside Judea. Simon had made a Passover pilgrimage to Jerusalem all the way from Cyrene in North Africa. His sons, Alexander and Rufus, are mentioned here probably because they became well known in the early church (Romans 16:13).

15:24 Throwing dice was a way of making a decision by chance. The soldiers gambled to decide who would receive Jesus' clothing.

Roman soldiers had the right to take for themselves the clothing of those crucified. This act fulfilled the prophecy of Psalm 22:18.

15:25 Crucifixion was a feared and shameful form of execution. The victim was forced to carry his cross along the longest possible route to the crucifixion site as a warning to bystanders. There were several shapes for crosses and several different methods of crucifixion. Jesus was nailed to the cross; condemned men were sometimes tied to their crosses with ropes. In either case, death came by suffocation as the person lost strength and the weight of the body made breathing more and more difficult.

him. 26A sign announced the charge against him. It read, "The King of the Jews." 27Two revolutionaries* were crucified with him, one on his right and one on his left.*

29The people passing by shouted abuse, shaking their heads in mockery. "Ha! Look at you now!" they yelled at him. "You said you were going to destroy the Temple and rebuild it in three days. 30Well then, save yourself and come down from the cross!"

15:29
Pss 22:7; 109:2
Mark 14:58
John 2:19

31The leading priests and teachers of religious law also mocked Jesus. "He saved others," they scoffed, "but he can't save himself! 32Let this Messiah, this King of Israel, come down from the cross so we can see it and believe him!" Even the men who were crucified with Jesus ridiculed him.

15:32
Zeph 3:15

Jesus Dies on the Cross (**236**/Matthew 27:45-56; Luke 23:44-49; John 19:28-37)
33At noon, darkness fell across the whole land until three o'clock. 34Then at three o'clock Jesus called out with a loud voice, *"Eloi, Eloi, lema sabachthani?"* which means "My God, my God, why have you abandoned me?"*

15:34
†Ps 22:1

35Some of the bystanders misunderstood and thought he was calling for the prophet Elijah. 36One of them ran and filled a sponge with sour wine, holding it up to him on a reed stick so he could drink. "Wait!" he said. "Let's see whether Elijah comes to take him down!"

15:36
Ps 69:21

37Then Jesus uttered another loud cry and breathed his last. 38And the curtain in the sanctuary of the Temple was torn in two, from top to bottom.

15:38
Exod 26:31-33
Heb 10:19-20

39When the Roman officer* who stood facing him* saw how he had died, he exclaimed, "This man truly was the Son of God!"

40Some women were there, watching from a distance, including Mary Magdalene, Mary (the mother of James the younger and of Joseph*), and Salome. 41They had been followers of Jesus and had cared for him while he was in Galilee. Many other women who had come with him to Jerusalem were also there.

15:40-41
Luke 8:2-3

Jesus Is Laid in the Tomb (**237**/Matthew 27:57-61; Luke 23:50-56; John 19:38-42)
42This all happened on Friday, the day of preparation,* the day before the Sabbath. As evening approached, 43Joseph of Arimathea took a risk and went to Pilate and asked for Jesus'

15:43
Luke 2:25, 38

15:27a Or *Two criminals.* **15:27b** Some manuscripts add verse 28, *And the Scripture was fulfilled that said, "He was counted among those who were rebels."* See Isa 53:12; also compare Luke 22:37. **15:34** Ps 22:1. **15:39a** Greek *the centurion;* similarly in 15:44, 45. **15:39b** Some manuscripts add *heard his cry and.* **15:40** Greek *Joses;* also in 15:47. See Matt 27:56. **15:42** Greek *It was the day of preparation.*

• **15:26** A sign stating the condemned man's crime was often placed on a cross as a warning. Because Jesus was never found guilty, the only accusation placed on his sign was the "crime" of being King of the Jews.

15:27 Luke records that one of these revolutionaries repented before his death, and Jesus promised that man that he would be with him in paradise (Luke 23:39-43).

• **15:31** Jesus could have saved himself, but he endured this suffering because of his love for us. He could have chosen not to take the pain and humiliation; he could have killed those who mocked him. But he suffered through it all because he loved even his enemies. We had a significant part in the drama that dark afternoon because our sins were on the cross, too. Jesus died on that cross for us, and the penalty for our sins was paid by his death. The only adequate response we can make is to confess our sins and gratefully accept the fact that Jesus paid for them so we wouldn't have to. Don't insult God with indifference toward the greatest act of genuine love in history.

15:32 When James and John had asked Jesus for the places of honor next to him in his Kingdom, Jesus had told them that they didn't know what they were asking (10:35-39). Here, as Jesus was preparing to inaugurate his Kingdom through his death, the places on his right and on his left were taken by dying men—criminals. As Jesus explained to his two power-hungry disciples, a person who wants to be close to Jesus must be prepared to suffer and die as he himself was doing. The way to the Kingdom is the way of the cross. If we want the glory of the Kingdom, we must be willing to be united with the crucified Christ.

15:34 Jesus did not ask this question in surprise or despair. He was quoting the first line of Psalm 22. The whole psalm is a prophecy expressing the deep agony of the Messiah's death for the world's sin. Jesus knew that he would be temporarily separated from God the moment he took upon himself the sins of the world. This separation was what he had dreaded as he prayed in Gethsemane. The physical agony was horrible, but the spiritual alienation from God was the ultimate torture.

15:37 Jesus' loud cry may have been his last words, "It is finished" (John 19:30).

15:38 A heavy curtain hung in front of the Temple room called the Most Holy Place, a place reserved by God for himself. Symbolically, the curtain separated the holy God from sinful people. The room was entered only once a year, on the Day of Atonement, by the high priest as he made a sacrifice to gain forgiveness for the sins of all the people. When Jesus died, the curtain was torn in two, showing that his death for our sins had opened up the way for us to approach our holy God. Read Hebrews 9 for a more complete explanation.

• **15:42ff** The Sabbath began at sundown on Friday and ended at sundown on Saturday. Jesus died just a few hours before sundown on Friday. It was against Jewish law to do physical work or to travel on the Sabbath. It was also against Jewish law to let a dead body remain exposed overnight (Deuteronomy 21:23). Joseph came to bury Jesus' body before the Sabbath began. If Jesus had died on the Sabbath when Joseph was unavailable, his body would have been taken down by the Romans. Had the Romans taken Jesus' body, no Jews could have confirmed his death, and opponents could have disputed his resurrection.

body. (Joseph was an honored member of the high council, and he was waiting for the Kingdom of God to come.) 44Pilate couldn't believe that Jesus was already dead, so he called for the Roman officer and asked if he had died yet. 45The officer confirmed that Jesus was dead, so Pilate told Joseph he could have the body. 46Joseph bought a long sheet of linen cloth. Then he took Jesus' body down from the cross, wrapped it in the cloth, and laid it in a tomb that had been carved out of the rock. Then he rolled a stone in front of the entrance. 47Mary Magdalene and Mary the mother of Joseph saw where Jesus' body was laid.

15:46
Acts 13:29

EVIDENCE THAT JESUS ACTUALLY DIED AND AROSE	*Proposed Explanations for Empty Tomb*	*Evidence against These Explanations*	*References*
This evidence demonstrates Jesus' uniqueness in history and proves that he is God's Son. No one else was able to predict his own resurrection and then accomplish it.	Jesus was only unconscious and later revived.	A Roman soldier told Pilate that Jesus was dead.	Mark 15:44, 45
		The Roman soldiers did not break Jesus' legs because he had already died, and one of them pierced Jesus' side with a spear.	John 19:32-34
		Joseph of Arimathea and Nicodemus wrapped Jesus' body and placed it in the tomb.	John 19:38-40
	The women made a mistake and went to the wrong tomb.	Mary Magdalene and Mary the mother of Joseph saw Jesus placed in the tomb.	Matthew 27:59-61 Mark 15:47 Luke 23:55
	Unknown thieves stole Jesus' body.	On Sunday morning Peter and John also went to the same tomb.	John 20:3-9
	The disciples stole Jesus' body.	The tomb was sealed and guarded by Roman soldiers.	Matthew 27:65, 66
		The disciples were ready to die for their faith. Stealing Jesus' body would have been admitting that their faith was meaningless.	Acts 12:2
	The religious leaders stole Jesus' body to produce it later.	If the religious leaders had taken Jesus' body, they would have produced it to stop the rumors of his resurrection.	None

15:42, 43 After Jesus died on the cross, Joseph of Arimathea asked for his body and then sealed it in a new tomb. Although an honored member of the high council, Joseph was a secret disciple of Jesus. Not all the Jewish leaders hated Jesus. Joseph risked his reputation to give a proper burial to his Lord. It is frightening to risk one's reputation even for what is right. If your Christian witness endangers your reputation, remember Joseph. Today he is remembered with admiration in the Christian church. How many other members of the Jewish high council can you name?

• **15:44** Pilate was surprised that Jesus had died so quickly, so he asked an officer to verify the report. Today, in an effort to deny the Resurrection, there are those who say that Jesus didn't really die. His death, however, was confirmed by the officer, Pilate, Joseph of Arimathea, the religious leaders, and the women who witnessed his burial. Jesus suffered actual physical death on the cross.

15:46 This tomb was probably a cave carved out from a hill. It was large enough to walk into. Joseph wrapped Jesus' body, placed it in the tomb, and rolled a heavy stone across the entrance. The religious leaders also watched where Jesus was buried. They stationed guards by the tomb and sealed the stone to make sure that no one would steal Jesus' body and claim he had risen from the dead (Matthew 27:62-66).

15:47 These women could do very little. They couldn't speak before the high council in Jesus' defense; they couldn't appeal to Pilate; they couldn't stand against the crowds; they couldn't overpower the Roman guards. But they did what they could.

They stayed at the cross when the disciples had fled, they followed Jesus' body to its tomb, and they prepared spices for his body. Because these women used the opportunities they had, they were the first to witness the Resurrection. God blessed their devotion and diligence. As believers, we should take advantage of the opportunities we have and do what we *can* for Christ, instead of worrying about what we cannot do.

Jesus Rises from the Dead (**239**/Matthew 28:1-7; Luke 24:1-12; John 20:1-10)

16 Saturday evening, when the Sabbath ended, Mary Magdalene, Mary the mother of James, and Salome went out and purchased burial spices so they could anoint Jesus' body. ²Very early on Sunday morning,* just at sunrise, they went to the tomb. ³On the way they were asking each other, "Who will roll away the stone for us from the entrance to the tomb?" ⁴But as they arrived, they looked up and saw that the stone, which was very large, had already been rolled aside.

⁵When they entered the tomb, they saw a young man clothed in a white robe sitting on the right side. The women were shocked, ⁶but the angel said, "Don't be alarmed. You are looking for Jesus of Nazareth,* who was crucified. He isn't here! He is risen from the dead! Look, this is where they laid his body. ⁷Now go and tell his disciples, including Peter, that Jesus is going ahead of you to Galilee. You will see him there, just as he told you before he died."

⁸The women fled from the tomb, trembling and bewildered, and they said nothing to anyone because they were too frightened.*

16:1
Luke 23:56
John 19:39-40
16:3
Mark 15:46

16:5
John 20:12
Acts 1:10; 10:30
16:6
Acts 2:23-32
1 Cor 15:4-12
16:7
Matt 26:32
John 21:1

[*Shorter Ending of Mark*]

Then they briefly reported all this to Peter and his companions. Afterward Jesus himself sent them out from east to west with the sacred and unfailing message of salvation that gives eternal life. Amen.

[*Longer Ending of Mark*]

Jesus Appears to Mary Magdalene (**240**/John 20:11-18)

⁹After Jesus rose from the dead early on Sunday morning, the first person who saw him was Mary Magdalene, the woman from whom he had cast out seven demons. ¹⁰She went to the disciples, who were grieving and weeping, and told them what had happened. ¹¹But when she told them that Jesus was alive and she had seen him, they didn't believe her.

16:9-11
Matt 28:1-10
John 20:11-18

Jesus Appears to Two Believers Traveling on the Road (**243**/Luke 24:13-34)

¹²Afterward he appeared in a different form to two of his followers who were walking from Jerusalem into the country. ¹³They rushed back to tell the others, but no one believed them.

16:12-13
Luke 24:13-35

16:2 Greek *on the first day of the week;* also in 16:9. **16:6** Or *Jesus the Nazarene.* **16:8** The most reliable early manuscripts of the Gospel of Mark end at verse 8. Other manuscripts include various endings to the Gospel. A few include both the "shorter ending" and the "longer ending." The majority of manuscripts include the "longer ending" immediately after verse 8.

16:1, 2 The women purchased the spices on Saturday evening after the Sabbath had ended so they could go to the tomb early the next morning and anoint Jesus' body as a sign of love, devotion, and respect. Bringing spices to the tomb was like bringing flowers to a grave today. These women faced two overwhelming problems as they set out to honor Jesus' body, however. The Roman guards and the huge rock in the tomb's doorway. Impossible obstacles. So what did these women expect to accomplish that early Sunday morning? Yet urged on by love and gratitude, they walked on—even as they wondered the same questions aloud.

The church's mission—to send the gospel to all the world—is fraught with overwhelming obstacles. Any one of them appears devastating. Against human stubbornness, disease, danger, terrorism, loneliness, sin, greed, and even church strife and corruption, what can a few missionaries hope to accomplish? Yet like these solitary women, we go out with love and gratitude for Jesus and leave the big obstacles to God.

16:5 Mark says that one angel met the women at the tomb, while Luke mentions two angels. Each Gospel writer chose to highlight different details as he explained the same story, just as eyewitnesses to a news story each may highlight a different aspect of that event. Mark probably emphasized only the angel who spoke. The unique emphasis of each Gospel shows that the four accounts were written independently. This should give us confidence that all four are true and reliable.

• **16:6** The Resurrection is vitally important for many reasons: (1) Jesus kept his promise to rise from the dead, so we can believe he will keep all his other promises. (2) The Resurrection ensures that the ruler of God's eternal Kingdom will be the living Christ, not just an idea, hope, or dream. (3) Christ's resurrection gives us the assurance that we also will be resurrected. (4) The power of God that brought Christ's body back from the dead is available to us to bring our morally and spiritually dead selves back to life so that we can change and grow (1 Corinthians 15:12-19). (5) The Resurrection provides the substance of the church's witness to the world. We do not merely tell lessons from the life of a good teacher; we proclaim the reality of the resurrection of Jesus Christ.

16:7 The angel made special mention of Peter to show that, in spite of Peter's denials, Jesus had not disowned or deserted him. Jesus had great responsibilities for Peter to fulfill in the church that was not yet in existence.

16:7 The angel told the disciples to meet Jesus in Galilee "as he told you" (see 14:28). This is where Jesus had called most of them and had said they would "fish for people" (Matthew 4:19), and it would be where this mission would be restated (John 21). But the disciples, filled with fear, remained behind locked doors in Jerusalem (John 20:19). Jesus met them first in Jerusalem (Luke 24:36) and later in Galilee (John 21). Then he returned to Jerusalem, where he ascended into heaven from the Mount of Olives (Acts 1:12).

Jesus Appears to Thomas (**245**/John 20:24-31)

16:14-18
Matt 28:16-20
Luke 24:36-49
John 20:19-23
Acts 1:6-8

[14]Still later he appeared to the eleven disciples as they were eating together. He rebuked them for their stubborn unbelief because they refused to believe those who had seen him after he had been raised from the dead.*

Jesus Gives the Great Commission (**248**/Matthew 28:16-20)

16:16
Acts 2:38;
16:31, 33
16:17
Acts 2:4, 11; 8:7;
10:46; 16:18; 19:6
16:18
Luke 10:19
Acts 28:3-6

[15]And then he told them, "Go into all the world and preach the Good News to everyone. [16]Anyone who believes and is baptized will be saved. But anyone who refuses to believe will be condemned. [17]These miraculous signs will accompany those who believe: They will cast out demons in my name, and they will speak in new languages.* [18]They will be able to handle snakes with safety, and if they drink anything poisonous, it won't hurt them. They will be able to place their hands on the sick, and they will be healed."

Jesus Ascends into Heaven (**250**/Luke 24:50-53)

16:19-20
Luke 24:50-53
Acts 1:9-11
16:19
Rom 8:34
Col 3:1
Heb 1:3

[19]When the Lord Jesus had finished talking with them, he was taken up into heaven and sat down in the place of honor at God's right hand. [20]And the disciples went everywhere and preached, and the Lord worked through them, confirming what they said by many miraculous signs.

16:14 Some early manuscripts add: *And they excused themselves, saying, "This age of lawlessness and unbelief is under Satan, who does not permit God's truth and power to conquer the evil [unclean] spirits. Therefore, reveal your justice now." This is what they said to Christ. And Christ replied to them, "The period of years of Satan's power has been fulfilled, but other dreadful things will happen soon. And I was handed over to death for those who have sinned, so that they may return to the truth and sin no more, and so they may inherit the spiritual, incorruptible, and righteous glory in heaven."* **16:17** Or *new tongues;* some manuscripts do not include *new.*

16:15 Jesus told his disciples to go into all the world, telling everyone that he had paid the penalty for sin and that those who believe in him can be forgiven and live eternally with God. Christians today in all parts of the world are telling this Good News to people who haven't heard about Christ. The driving power that carries missionaries around the world and sets Christ's church in motion is the faith that comes from the Resurrection. Do you ever feel as though you don't have the skill or determination to be a witness for Christ? You must personally realize that Jesus rose from the dead and lives for you today. As you grow in your relationship with Christ, he will give you both the opportunities and the inner strength to tell his message.

16:16 It is not the water of baptism that saves but God's grace accepted through faith in Christ. Because of Jesus' response to the criminal on the cross who died with him, we know it is possible to be saved without being baptized (Luke 23:43). Baptism alone, without faith, does not guarantee that a person will go to heaven. Those who refuse to accept Jesus as their Savior will be condemned, regardless of whether or not they have been baptized.

16:18 There are times when God intervenes miraculously to protect his followers. Occasionally he gives them special powers.

Paul handled a snake safely (Acts 28:5), and the disciples healed the sick (Matthew 10:1; Acts 3:7, 8). This does not mean, however, that we should test God by putting ourselves in dangerous situations or try to tempt the laws of nature. No one should build a religion on a portion of Scripture. God calls us to live as new citizens in the eternal Kingdom and to witness by word and service to God's love and power. Our witness should center on Jesus, not on superhero-type stunts.

16:19 When Jesus ascended into heaven, his physical presence left the disciples (Acts 1:9). Jesus' sitting at God's right hand signifies the completion of his work, his authority as God, and his coronation as King.

16:20 Mark's Gospel emphasizes Christ's power as well as his servanthood. Jesus' life and teaching turned the world upside down and continue to do so. The world sees power as a way to gain control over others. But Jesus, with all authority and power in heaven and earth, chose to serve others. He held children in his arms, healed the sick, washed the disciples' feet, and died for the sins of the world. Jesus' followers today receive this same power to serve. As believers, we are called to be servants of Christ. As Christ served, so we are to serve.

STUDY QUESTIONS

Thirteen lessons for individual or group study

HOW TO USE THIS BIBLE STUDY

It's always exciting to get more than you expect. And that's what you'll find in this Bible study guide—much more than you expect. Our goal was to write thoughtful, practical, dependable, and application-oriented studies of God's word.

This study guide contains the complete text of the selected Bible book. The commentary is accurate, complete, and loaded with unique charts, maps, and profiles of Bible people.

With the Bible text, extensive notes and features, and questions to guide discussion, Life Application Bible Studies have everything you need in one place.

The lessons in this Bible-study guide will work for large classes as well as small-group studies. To get everyone involved in your discussions, encourage participants to answer the questions before each meeting.

Each lesson is divided into five easy-to-lead sections. The section called "Reflect" introduces you and the members of your group to a specific area of life touched by the lesson. "Read" shows which chapters to read and which notes and other features to use. Additional questions help you understand the passage. "Realize" brings into focus the biblical principle to be learned with questions, a special insight, or both. "Respond" helps you make connections with your own situation and personal needs. The questions are designed to help you find areas in your life where you can apply the biblical truths. "Resolve" helps you map out action plans for that day.

Begin and end each lesson with prayer, asking for the Holy Spirit's guidance, direction, and wisdom.

Recommended time allotments for each section of a lesson are as follows:

Segment	60 minutes	90 minutes
Reflect on your life	5 minutes	10 minutes
Read the passage	10 minutes	15 minutes
Realize the principle	15 minutes	20 minutes
Respond to the message	20 minutes	30 minutes
Resolve to take action	10 minutes	15 minutes

All five sections work together to help a person learn the lessons, live out the principles, and obey the commands taught in the Bible.

Also, at the end of each lesson, there is a section entitled "More for studying other themes in this section." These questions will help you lead the group in studying other parts of each section not covered in depth by the main lesson.

But don't just listen to God's word. You must do what it says. Otherwise, you are only fooling yourselves. For if you listen to the word and don't obey, it is like glancing at your face in a mirror. You see yourself, walk away, and forget what you look like. But if you look carefully into the perfect law that sets you free, and if you do what it says and don't forget what you heard, then God will bless you for doing it (James 1:22-25).

LESSON 1
MARK: ACTION PACKED!
MARK INTRODUCTION

REFLECT
on your life

1 Without reading ahead, jot down all you know about Mark the man and Mark the Gospel.

_____

_____

_____

_____

_____

READ
the passage

Read the introductory material to Mark and the following notes:

❏ 1:1   ❏ 1:2-4

2 Why is the Gospel of Mark considered a book of action?

_____

_____

_____

_____

3 How does this book compare to an action-packed, best-selling novel that you might find in a bookstore?

_____

_____

_____

4 What are the similarities between the Roman world of Mark's day and our world today?

_____

_____

_____

_____

5 Look again at the Megathemes. How would you rate your life in the following areas?

Megatheme	Poorly		OK		Well
Servant: How am I doing in serving others?	1	2	3	4	5
Spreading the Gospel: How is my evangelism?	1	2	3	4	5

6 Why do so many people today read the Bible and believe that it is true, yet stumble at applying it completely to their lives?

_____

_____

_____

_____

_____

Mark is an action-packed book. It portrays Jesus as a man of action—he got things done when and how they needed to be done. The first words of Christ recorded in this book carry a profound message: " 'The time promised by God has come at last!' he announced. 'The Kingdom of God is near! Repent of your sins and believe the Good News!' " (Mark 1:15). All too often those in church tend to hear the words but fail to act on them. Acquiring knowledge without acting on what we learn leads to a fruitless and dull faith and, ultimately, pride and hypocrisy. But when we begin to act on the commands and principles of Scripture, our walk with Christ becomes heartfelt and productive. To know what is right and not do it is sin. A small change each day will add up to a changed life.

7 How would you rate yourself in terms of obeying what the Bible teaches?

_____

_____

_____

_____

_____

8 What hinders you from living out a truth you have learned from the Bible?

_____

_____

_____

_____

_____

_____

_____

9 Obeying God and taking action is more difficult in certain areas of our life than in others. In which area of your life would you most like to become more of a person of action?

_____

_____

_____

_____

_____

_____

RESOLVE
to take action

10 Pray each day this week that God would help you become a person who takes action—one who hears and obeys. When is the best time of day for you to make this regular request to God in prayer?

_____

_____

_____

_____

11 How can you remind yourself to do it?

_____

_____

_____

_____

_____

_____

A In what ways was the audience of this Gospel different from those of the other three Gospels?

B If you had been writing an account of the life of Christ for the Romans, name the ten most significant events that you would have wanted to include.

C How can you serve others at home? on the job? at school? in your neighborhood? at church?

MORE
for studying
other themes
in this section

LESSON 2
REDUCING YOUR THREAT LEVEL
MARK 1:1–2:28

REFLECT
on your life

1 What picture comes to mind when you hear the word *Pharisee? dress? lifestyle? attitudes?*

_____

_____

_____

_____

_____

READ
the passage

Read Mark 1:1–2:28 and the following notes:

❒ 1:5 ❒ 1:12, 13 ❒ 1:17 ❒ 1:21 ❒ 1:21, 22 ❒ 1:23, 24 ❒ 1:29-31

❒ 1:32, 33 ❒ 1:35-37 ❒ 1:39 ❒ 1:40, 41 ❒ 2:3 ❒ 2:4 ❒ 2:14

❒ 2:16, 17 ❒ 2:18ff ❒ 2:22 ❒ 2:23 ❒ 2:24

2 List all of the people mentioned in these first two chapters and place them on this chart as open and receptive, cautious and uncertain, or closed and suspicious toward Christ and his message (1:1–2:28).

Open and Receptive	Cautious and Uncertain	Closed and Suspicious
_____	_____	_____
_____	_____	_____
_____	_____	_____
_____	_____	_____
_____	_____	_____

3 If you had been from a family of struggling fishermen and had been in the crowd at this time, how would you have responded to Christ and his message (receptive, uncertain, or suspicious)?

_____

_____

_____

4 If you had been a leader in a local synagogue or from a prosperous family, and had been in the crowd at this time, how would you have responded to Christ and his message (receptive, uncertain, or suspicious)?

_____

_____

_____

5 Why do you suppose the religious leaders—the very ones who should have been the first to recognize Jesus as the Messiah—were threatened by his teaching and miracles?

REALIZE
the principle

_____

_____

_____

_____

_____

In these two chapters we see a dramatic contrast between those who felt hopeful and those who felt threatened. On the one hand, the fishermen immediately left their nets to follow Jesus, leaving their occupation and livelihood behind. On the other hand, many of the religious leaders began to criticize Jesus for differing with their viewpoint and ignoring certain religious customs. Today Jesus still receives a mixed reaction, and many people still feel threatened by him. How do you respond to Jesus?

6 Why do some unbelievers feel threatened by the church, the Bible, and Christians?

_____

_____

_____

_____

_____

7 Why do some Christians feel threatened by the teachings in the Bible or by the faithful lives of other Christians?

_____

_____

_____

_____

8 Making a positive change can be difficult. Why is it even more difficult to face change or to make a change in the spiritual area of our life?

_____

_____

_____

_____

RESPOND
to the message

9 In what areas (home, school, work, church, neighborhood) do you feel most like the fishermen—immediately ready to drop what you are doing and follow Christ? (In other words, in what areas are you most willing to give things up for Christ?)

_____

_____

_____

_____

10 In what areas (home, school, work, church, neighborhood) are you slower to respond—perhaps even feeling threatened by the changes that God may want to make in your life?

_____

_____

_____

11 What steps can you take to become more responsive to what God wants to be and to do in your life?

_____

_____

_____

_____

12 Select one area of your life in which you feel embarrassed, hesitant, or threatened when you think about submitting it to the Lord. Begin by writing down your feelings of fear and the reasons for your reluctance to change. Then pray about them during the week—tell God how you feel.

_____

_____

_____

_____

_____

13 To help you feel more comfortable about this area, go to God in prayer. Ask the Lord to give you a willing heart to obey him fully, immediately, and unreservedly in this area of your life.

A Why was this exactly the right time for Jesus to come?

B Why did John the Baptist dress the way he did?

C How did John the Baptist prepare the way for Jesus? How can you prepare to meet Jesus and prepare others to meet him?

D Why was it important for Jesus to be baptized?

E How was Jesus prepared for his ministry?

F Why did Jesus spend so much of his ministry time in Galilee instead of Jerusalem?

G How was Jesus able to preach in many synagogues when the religious leaders were so suspicious of him?

H What kinds of people did Jesus help? What kinds of people need Christ's help today? How can you bring them to Christ?

I Why wasn't it against the Sabbath law for Jesus and the disciples to pick the grain?

J Why was Jesus criticized for eating with tax collectors?

K How did Jesus pose a threat to each of the Jewish religious and political groups listed in the chart in question 2?

LESSON 3
EXCUSES DON'T WORK
MARK 3:1-35

REFLECT
on your life

1 Think back to when you were young and you tried to get out of doing something you were supposed to do, like a chore around the house or an assignment at school. What tactics did you use to try to get out of it?

_____

_____

_____

READ
the passage

Read Mark 3:1-35 and the following notes:

❐ 3:6   ❐ 3:7-11   ❐ 3:14   ❐ 3:21   ❐ 3:31-35

2 The Pharisees and supporters of Herod did not normally work well together. Why then did they cooperate against Jesus (3:6)?

_____

_____

_____

_____

3 Why would a young man at this time want to follow Jesus and become one of his disciples (3:13-19)?

_____

_____

_____

_____

4 If you had been among the crowds watching Jesus, how willing would you have been to side with him, identify with him, and become known as one of his followers?

_____

_____

_____

_____

While large crowds followed Jesus, not everyone wanted to be known as his follower. Some sought to be healed, and others were merely curious or interested in getting some firsthand information about this controversial figure. To become known as one of his followers would be costly. A follower might incur the wrath of the religious and political leaders of the nation, not to mention the disdain of some relatives and friends. Following Jesus will cost us as well. At times we want to avoid the disdain of family, friends, and acquaintances— there is no benefit in being known as a religious fanatic. Yet if we avoid identifying with Christ at all cost, we will be unable to serve him.

5 If a reporter interviewed people in a shopping mall for the evening news, what would they say about those who want to be followers of Christ?

_____

_____

_____

_____

6 How would you rate your willingness to be known as a follower of Christ?

_____

_____

_____

_____

_____

7 In what ways do you feel underqualified to be a disciple of Jesus?

_____

_____

_____

_____

8 If Jesus were selecting disciples today, what excuses would you be tempted to use for not following him? Why?

_____

_____

_____

_____

_____

_____

_____

R
RESOLVE
to take action

9 In what situations are you most afraid to identify with Christ? When are you most embarrassed to be known as a Christian?

_____

_____

_____

_____

_____

_____

10 List the excuses or tactics you tend to use to avoid being known as a Christian. Pray that you will stop using them and have the courage to identify with Christ.

_____

_____

_____

_____

_____

_____

_____

MORE
for studying
other themes
in this section

A Why did Jesus choose twelve men?

B Look at the chart entitled "The Twelve Disciples." Which of the lessons from their lives is the most meaningful for you?

C Why did the crowds follow Jesus? Why did the disciples follow him? Why do you follow Christ?

D What evidence is given for Jesus' divinity? How did the religious teachers explain his power (3:22)? How do people explain Christ today?

E Who are Christ's brothers and sisters? On what basis can a person count himself/herself as one of them?

LESSON 4
THE FOUR SOILS
MARK 4:1-41

REFLECT
on your life

1 What are some steps to having a productive garden?

_____

_____

_____

_____

READ
the passage

Read Mark 4:1-41 and the following notes:

❐ 4:2   ❐ 4:3   ❐ 4:9   ❐ 4:14-20   ❐ 4:24, 25

2 What plants are you familiar with that yield thirty, sixty, or one hundred times what was planted?

_____

_____

_____

_____

3 Why would a good farmer throw good seed onto poor soil?

_____

_____

_____

_____

_____

4 What is the main point of this parable (4:14-20)?

_____

_____

_____

_____

_____

_____

REALIZE
the principle

5 Today only a small percentage of the population are farmers, and many people are not even gardeners. What are some other situations in which people expect a good return for their efforts?

_____

_____

_____

_____

_____

_____

Most readers of this parable quickly classify themselves as one of the four types of soils and move on. But rarely will good farmers judge their land that hastily. They will be careful to note the different types of soil on the land. They will be aware of gradual changes over time and then rotate crops accordingly. When we give our life this same level of attention, we soon see that our heart can be a combination of the soils in the parable. Some areas are more fertile and open to God's will than others. Some areas deteriorate over time. It can be quite revealing to examine our life plot by plot, piece by piece.

6 Note the approximate times in your life when you would describe yourself as each of these types of soil.

RESPOND
to the message

Age	Hard	Rocky	Thorny	Good
___	___	___	___	___
___	___	___	___	___
___	___	___	___	___
___	___	___	___	___
___	___	___	___	___
___	___	___	___	___

7 Roughly divide your life into the following categories: family, friends, faith, finances, and future. How would you describe the soil of your life in each of these areas?

	Hard	Rocky	Thorny	Good
Family (spouse, children, parents)	_____	_____	_____	_____
Friends (neighbors, coworkers)	_____	_____	_____	_____
Faith (prayer, worship, evangelism)	_____	_____	_____	_____
Finances (income, debt, stewardship)	_____	_____	_____	_____
Future (career plans, hope, worry)	_____	_____	_____	_____

RESOLVE
to take action

8 Choose one area of your life, and list two or three steps you can take to improve the condition of the soil there. How can you weed it? remove rocks? plow it? fertilize it?

_____

_____

_____

_____

_____

_____

_____

MORE
for studying
other themes
in this section

A How is it that people today can hear the good news of salvation and refuse to accept it?

B Why did Jesus spend so much of his time telling stories when he taught the large crowds?

C How does putting into practice what we know help us to understand more about God's Kingdom? What will happen if we do not put our knowledge into practice?

D How did Jesus teach his disciples? How does he teach us today? How can you teach others about him?

E What do you know about the Kingdom of God from the parables in this chapter?

F Why were the disciples afraid in the boat? How did Jesus react to the storm? How could the disciples have interpreted Jesus' sleeping? What does it mean for you to have confidence in Christ?

LESSON 5
THE TOUCH OF JESUS
MARK 5:1-43

REFLECT
on your life

1 When have you felt rejected by others?

_____

_____

_____

_____

2 What groups of people are considered rejects by our society?

_____

_____

_____

_____

READ
the passage

Read Mark 5:1-43 and the following notes:

❒ 5:11   ❒ 5:19, 20   ❒ 5:25-34   ❒ 5:39, 40   ❒ 5:41, 42

3 Why would most people in Jesus' time want to avoid coming in contact with a woman who was hemorrhaging (5:25)?

_____

_____

_____

_____

_____

4 In this chapter what kinds of social barriers do you see Jesus breaking through?

_____

_____

_____

_____

Jesus surprised the people of his day by reaching out to social outcasts. We see dramatic examples of this in chapter 5. People with running sores and those who had been in recent contact with a dead body were considered unclean and were to be avoided. Religious people today are often surprised to learn about the kinds of people they should reach out and touch. Sometimes we don't want to go near such people. Sometimes we don't know what to do or are unintentionally condescending when we try to help. Jesus shows us how to live lives motivated by compassion. The example Jesus set eliminates our excuses for allowing any barrier to separate us from those in need. No person is beyond Christ's loving touch.

REALIZE
the principle

5 Look at the chart entitled "The Touch of Jesus." Then draw some contemporary parallels between the outcasts of Jesus' day and the outcasts of our day as illustrated below:

Then	Now
A despised tax collector	An IRS agent
An outcast with leprosy	A person with AIDS

_____   _____

_____   _____

_____   _____

_____   _____

_____   _____

_____   _____

6 In what ways are you like any of the groups of people on this list?

_____

_____

_____

_____

RESPOND
to the message

7 Which kinds of people on this list are fairly easy and natural for you to reach out to?

_____

_____

_____

_____

8 Which kinds of people do you find difficult to reach out to?

_____

_____

_____

_____

9 With which of these groups of rejected people do you have some kind of contact?

_____

_____

_____

10 What are some creative ways that you can show care and concern for them?

_____

_____

_____

_____

_____

RESOLVE
to take action

11 Find a way soon to reach out to someone you know who feels rejected and perhaps might even be an outcast in society. How could you show this person God's love?

_____

_____

_____

_____

A Why were the demons so afraid of Jesus? Who did the demons say Jesus was? Why is this significant?

B Why were the people of this region afraid of Jesus after he had healed this man?

C Why would Jesus tell the man he healed to spread the news and yet tell the parents not to tell anyone that he had brought their daughter back to life?

D Why was Jesus so concerned that the woman know it was her faith that had healed her?

E Does God still heal people today? How would you like him to heal you?

MORE
for studying
other themes
in this section

LESSON 6
COPING WITH CRITICISM
MARK 6:1-56

REFLECT
on your life

1 How do you tend to react when people disagree with you?

_____

_____

_____

_____

_____

_____

READ
the passage

Read Mark 6:1-56, the profile of Herod Antipas, and the following notes:

❏ 6:11   ❏ 6:14, 15   ❏ 6:17-19   ❏ 6:20   ❏ 6:22, 23

2 What was God's message to Herod through John the Baptist?

_____

_____

_____

_____

_____

_____

REALIZE
the principle

Although Herod had thrown John into prison as a favor to Herodias, he still respected John. Herodias, on the other hand, thoroughly hated John for criticizing her marriage and wasn't satisfied until she had him killed. Today many people still cannot handle criticism. But the problem is that sometimes there is a kernel of truth in the unfavorable comments of others, and God has something for us to learn. If we carefully evaluate criticism that comes our way and pray about it, we won't miss the lesson to be learned.

3 What public figures can you think of who have lately demonstrated an unwillingness to accept criticism?

_____

_____

_____

_____

_____

4 What bothers you the most about another person's criticism of you?

_____

RESPOND
to the message

_____

_____

_____

_____

_____

_____

5 When in the past have you received criticism that really hurt but turned out to be very instructive and helpful for you?

_____

_____

_____

_____

_____

_____

6 Reevaluate what someone has told you recently about your life. What did this person say that you can take to heart?

_____

_____

_____

_____

_____

_____

7 Sometimes we are not open to criticism from those who are closest to us. Who are some of the people who tell you things you need to hear but sometimes ignore? From whom else is it difficult for you to receive criticism?

_____

_____

_____

_____

_____

_____

_____

RESOLVE
to take action

8 Think about some possible criticism you may face this week. How do you want to react to it? What creative steps can help you respond appropriately?

_____

_____

_____

_____

_____

_____

_____

MORE
for studying
other themes
in this section

A Why were the people of Nazareth angry at Jesus? Why was it so difficult for them to believe in him? Who is like this toward you?

B Why did Jesus send out the disciples? Why did Jesus tell the disciples to travel without any extra supplies for their trip? What tasks does God ask you to do without a safety net?

C List the principles of witnessing implied by 6:1-13. How can you use these principles?

D Why were there so many differing opinions about the identity of Jesus? Who knew best who Jesus was? In what ways can your life be like theirs?

E What did the disciples learn from watching Jesus feed people, walk on water, and heal the sick (see 6:52)? What can we learn about Christ?

F Why were people following Jesus at this point in his ministry? How do their reasons and motives compare with those of people today who consider themselves Christians?

LESSON 7
GOING THROUGH THE MOTIONS
MARK 7:1–9:1

REFLECT
on your life

1 What do people usually mean when they call someone a hypocrite?

_____

_____

_____

_____

READ
the passage

Read Mark 7:1–9:1 and the following notes:

❐ 7:1ff ❐ 7:3, 4 ❐ 7:6, 7 ❐ 7:8, 9 ❐ 7:10, 11 ❐ 7:18, 19 ❐ 8:11 ❐ 8:34

2 Why did Jesus call the Pharisees hypocrites (7:6-13)?

_____

_____

_____

_____

REALIZE
the principle

3 The Pharisees were caught up in observing religious externals with little concern for inner purity. What are the externals in your church that people may use to judge others?

_____

_____

_____

_____

_____

It's easy to catch ourselves just going through the motions in our worship and church life. At times we all find ourselves singing hymns without paying attention to the words, or giving the right answers in Bible study without concern for putting the truths into practice. This is when we are in danger of lapsing into hypocrisy. All that is lacking is the *intention* of making people think that we are something that we are not. But trying to live a Christian life when our faith is weak is not hypocrisy. Satan uses our fear of being called a hypocrite to keep us passive. Never be afraid to live a vibrant Christian life. When you find yourself beginning to go through the motions, don't give up or put up a false front. Instead, fan the flame back into a roaring fire.

4 How can people restore meaning and significance to their faith when they find themselves beginning to go through the motions?

_____

_____

_____

_____

_____

_____

_____

5 When are you tempted to exaggerate what's happening in your life—either good or bad?

RESPOND
to the message

_____

_____

_____

_____

_____

6 In what aspects of your Christian life have you been more concerned about your image at church than about the inner reality of your heart?

_____

_____

_____

_____

_____

7 How have you been paralyzed by the fear of being labeled a hypocrite?

_____

_____

_____

_____

_____

8 Usually it's easy to spot hypocrisy in others but difficult to see it in ourselves. Who might think that *you* are a hypocrite?

_____

_____

_____

_____

R
RESOLVE
to take action

9 In what areas would you like to be free from fear so that you can serve God more wholeheartedly?

_____

_____

_____

_____

10 In areas where you have been trying to make others think you are something you are not, pray for humility. What would you like to be able to stop doing?

_____

_____

_____

MORE
for studying
other themes
in this section

A Why did Jesus spend such a large percentage of his time with the Jews as compared to the Gentiles? If he was so concerned about the Jews, why did he give any of his precious time to the Gentiles?

B Why did the disciples have difficulty understanding what Jesus was teaching? Which of his teachings are most difficult for you to understand? Why?

C Would the religious leaders have been convinced that Jesus is God's Son had he provided a sign from heaven? Why were they asking for something from heaven rather than something from earth (8:11)?

D Why do you think Jesus responded in the ways he did to the woman from Syrian Phoenicia and to the deaf man (7:25-29, 32-36)? Why did he perform these healings?

E Why were the people amazed at Jesus' miracles? What would it take to amaze you? What is his greatest miracle?

F How could more than four thousand people end up in the wilderness with no food to eat (8:1, 9)? What can you learn about the disciples from their response to Jesus' concern for the hungry crowd (8:4)? In what ways can you reflect greater faith than they did?

G What does it take to convince people that Christ is who he claims to be (see 8:12)? How can you be a part of that process?

H Why did Jesus touch the blind man two times (8:22-25)? What did Jesus tell him to do afterward (8:26)? Why?

I Compare Peter's words in 8:29 and 8:32 (also compare Jesus' response in 8:30 and 8:33). Why was there such a difference between Peter's and Jesus' words (8:33)? In what ways do we copy Peter's mistake? What can help us avoid doing this?

J What does it mean to follow Christ (8:34)? How can you keep close to him?

LESSON 8
THE EYES OF FAITH
MARK 9:2–10:52

REFLECT
on your life

1 What would you list as your three most expensive possessions, your two most important relationships, and your most valuable position?

_____

_____

_____

_____

_____

READ
the passage

Read Mark 9:2–10:52 and the following notes:

❏ 9:3ff   ❏ 9:9, 10   ❏ 9:12, 13   ❏ 9:34   ❏ 9:41, 42   ❏ 10:13-16
❏ 10:17-23   ❏ 10:37   ❏ 10:42-45   ❏ 10:47

2 Why did the disciples find it difficult to understand Jesus when he spoke about rising from the dead (9:30-32)?

_____

_____

_____

_____

3 How could the disciples lapse into an argument about personal greatness at such an important time in their lives and with such an important person in their midst (9:33-34)?

_____

_____

_____

4 Not everyone who wanted to believe in Jesus was asked to sell his/her possessions. Why did Jesus ask it of the rich man (10:21)?

_____

_____

_____

_____

5 What might have motivated James and John to ask for a special place and special treatment in God's Kingdom (10:35-37)?

_____

_____

_____

_____

6 How could the blind man have found out about the coming Messiah since he could not read, and about Jesus of Nazareth since he could not see (10:46-47)?

_____

_____

_____

_____

Wrong expectations prevented people from seeing who Jesus really is. Many of the Jews were expecting a conquering king, not a suffering servant. The disciples could not see him clearly, and the religious leaders were blind to his identity. But the blind man recognized Jesus for who he was. We also have expectations that prevent us from seeing Jesus clearly—expectations about the way God will work in the world, the way he will work in our life, and the position and power he will grant us here on earth. Like the disciples, we need to examine our expectations and take a fresh look at Jesus through the eyes of faith.

REALIZE
the principle

7 Wrong expectations blinded many Jews to Jesus' identity. What expectations do you have of him that could keep you from seeing who he really is?

_____

_____

_____

_____

RESPOND
to the message

8 What false expectations are you holding on to? What views are you secretly afraid of changing?

_____

_____

_____

_____

9 What are you trying to control or possess that Jesus may ask you to give up?

_____

_____

_____

_____

10 What might you see if you took a new look at Jesus and a new look at the way you are living your life?

_____

_____

_____

_____

RESOLVE
to take action

11 As we progress through life, from time to time we need to stop and take a new look at Jesus. The more life experiences we have, the more we can see in Christ's life that is relevant to ours. How can you take a new look at Jesus at this time in your life?

_____

_____

_____

_____

MORE
for studying
other themes
in this section

A Why is the transfiguration of Jesus important for us (9:2-13)?

B If the disciples had driven out demons before, why couldn't they drive one out of the demon-possessed boy (9:14-29)?

C Why were the disciples afraid to ask Jesus what he meant about his death (9:32)?

D Why would the disciples not want other people to use Jesus' name to work miracles (9:38)? What do Christians do today that is similar?

E How do Jesus' statements in 9:43-50 relate to the temptations we face today?

F Why is the teaching about marriage and divorce recorded in 10:2-12 so difficult for many people to accept today? What is God's ideal for marriage? What are the primary causes of most divorces?

G How might a church unintentionally discourage little children from coming to Christ (see 10:13-16)?

H How can you reflect Christ's values in your relationships with your loved ones?

I In what ways can a person be rich (10:17-31)? How can *your* riches keep you from God? What sacrifice might enable you to follow Christ more closely?

J When have you seen outstanding examples of leaders serving others (10:45)? What are some examples you have seen or experienced of leaders lording it over others (10:42)?

K What does it mean to be a "slave of everyone else" (10:44)? How can you serve others?

LESSON 9
BRINGING YOURSELF UNDER AUTHORITY
MARK 11:1-33

R

REFLECT
on your life

1 What items do you have with you that signify your authority or your submission to an authority?

_____

_____

_____

_____

_____

R

READ
the passage

Read Mark 11:1-33 and the following notes:

❑ 11:1, 2   ❑ 11:9, 10   ❑ 11:15-17   ❑ 11:22, 23   ❑ 11:27-33

2 What authority did the people ascribe to Jesus by their actions (11:8-10)?

_____

_____

_____

_____

3 How could Jesus clear the Temple when he held no man-made position of authority over the merchants (11:15-17)?

_____

_____

_____

_____

4 What authority do we have when we pray (11:20-25)?

_____

_____

_____

_____

5 By what authority did the religious leaders challenge Jesus' authority (11:27-33)?

_____

_____

_____

_____

As Jesus rode into Jerusalem, the people praised him but did not place them-selves under his authority. In the Temple the religious leaders not only refused to submit but also questioned his authority. Many people today pay homage to Jesus without submitting to his authority. They applaud him loudly but do not do what he says; they have a religion without substance and offer worship without service. Responding to Christ's authority means not only proclaiming his lordship but also obeying his commands.

REALIZE
the principle

6 If Jesus were to "clean house" at your church, what kinds of changes do you think he would make?

_____

_____

_____

_____

_____

_____

7 How can some people loudly defend the inerrancy of the Bible but have little or no concern for its authority in their lives?

_____

_____

_____

8 Where might Jesus want to "clean house" in your life?

RESPOND
to the message

_____

_____

_____

_____

_____

_____

9 List specific decisions, actions, or areas in your life where you give full, limited, or no authority to God.

Full Authority	*Limited Authority*	*No Authority*
_____	_____	_____
_____	_____	_____
_____	_____	_____
_____	_____	_____
_____	_____	_____
_____	_____	_____

10 What keeps you from submitting more completely to the lordship of Christ?

_____

_____

_____

_____

_____

11 As an experiment, take one of the areas you listed under "Limited Authority" or "No Authority" and pray for the willingness and courage to allow God to rule over this area of your life. Which area is the most important for you to work on at this time?

RESOLVE
to take action

_____

_____

_____

_____

A Why did the people hail Jesus as their king (11:1-11)? What did they expect him to do?

MORE
for studying
other themes
in this section

B What place is there for anger in the life of a Christian (11:12-17)? What makes you angry?

C What do you pray about? List recent answers to your prayers. Why doesn't God say yes to all our prayer requests?

D Jesus challenged the authority of the religious leaders (11:18, 27-28). Whose authority is challenged by Jesus today?

LESSON 10
WATCH OUT FOR TRAPS
MARK 12:1-44

R

REFLECT
on your life

1 How are you a spiritual leader at church? in your neighborhood? at work?

_____

_____

_____

_____

_____

_____

_____

R

READ
the passage

Read Mark 12:1-44 and the following notes:

❐ 12:14   ❐ 12:17   ❐ 12:18-23   ❐ 12:28   ❐ 12:38-40

2 If you had lived in Jerusalem at this time, would you have favored the Pharisees? the Sadducees? the supporters of Herod?

_____

_____

_____

R

REALIZE
the principle

3 Who are the religious leaders of our day and our society?

_____

_____

_____

_____

In this chapter, the religious leaders, infuriated by a parable, tried to trap Jesus with several well-thought-out trick questions and were embarrassed when unable to answer Jesus' question. While it's easy to be appalled at the attitude of those religious leaders, the fact is that we may have the same tendencies. It is easy to become embroiled in theological arguments and ignore or forget the purposes and power of God. We may feel threatened by what the Scriptures are saying about certain areas of our life. And we may pretend to be interested in spiritual things in order to keep up good appearances. While correct doctrine is important, we should not use it as a weapon, setting traps and roadblocks for those who are trying to do God's work.

4 The question about the resurrection was an issue that sharply divided the Pharisees and Sadducees. What thorny issues or theological questions divide believers in a similar way today?

_____

_____

_____

_____

_____

_____

5 The religious leaders became furious at the implications of the story of the evil farmers (12:1-12). What kinds of accusations would make you furious?

_____

RESPOND
to the message

_____

_____

_____

_____

_____

6 Many of the Pharisees pretended to be pious. In what ways do you pretend to be something you are not?

_____

_____

_____

_____

_____

_____

7 Teachers of the law craved recognition and honor. In what ways do you seek recognition and honor?

_____

_____

_____

_____

_____

_____

RESOLVE
to take action

8 Ask God to make you sensitive to his purposes and plans so that you do not become a hindrance to those who are genuinely trying to do God's work. If you had to select one, what kind of trap are you most inclined to set for others?

_____

_____

_____

_____

_____

MORE
for studying
other themes
in this section

A Why would Jesus tell a parable that was sure to infuriate the religious leaders (12:1-12)?

B What arguments were used to try to trick Jesus (12:13-15, 19-23, 28)? What do Jesus' answers tell us about him (12:15-17, 24-27, 29-34)?

C Whom do you know who is not far from the Kingdom of God (12:34)? How can you help bring that person closer?

D The religious leaders were more interested in the technicalities of their laws than in loving God and their neighbor. When do you tend to get caught up in rules and forget about people?

E Why did Jesus commend the poor widow for her gift (12:43-44)? What aspect of her example does Jesus want us to copy? What are some ways you could do this?

LESSON 11
BE PREPARED
MARK 13:1-37

REFLECT
on your life

1 Think of an area of life where preparation is important (for example, public speaking, cooking, teaching, woodworking, test taking, vacationing, and so on). What steps do you have to take to be prepared?

_____

_____

_____

_____

2 How can you prepare for Christ's return?

_____

_____

_____

_____

_____

READ
the passage

Read Mark 13:1-37 and the following notes:

❑ 13:3ff ❑ 13:5-7 ❑ 13:13 ❑ 13:32 ❑ 13:33, 34 ❑ 13:35-37

3 What do you think was going through the disciples' minds when they heard Jesus talking about the Temple being destroyed and the other events of the last days (13:5-37)?

_____

_____

_____

_____

_____

4 Has anyone ever asked you to watch or guard something for a period of time? Was it difficult to remain alert or easy to become distracted?

_____

_____

_____

_____

The intent of this passage is not to make us fearful but to give us hope and to help us remain alert. When we look around us at the sin in the world, it's easy to lose hope. But the promise of Christ's second coming reassures us. When we look around at the pleasures in the world, it is easy to become preoccupied or sidetracked from our mission. But the promise of Christ's second coming keeps us alert. Spiritual preparedness should be among our highest priorities. How we live each day matters very much. This means we should do nothing that we would regret if this were the last hour of our life.

5 How does the message in this chapter give us hope when everything seems to be going wrong?

_____

_____

_____

_____

_____

6 What people are most happy to hear about the second coming of Christ?

_____

_____

_____

_____

7 How can some Christians be fascinated by events preceding the second coming of Christ and yet not want to prepare for it?

_____

_____

_____

_____

_____

8 What frightens you most about the end times?

_____

_____

_____

_____

_____

9 What is most difficult about waiting for Christ to return?

_____

_____

_____

_____

_____

10 What do you want to be doing when Christ returns?

_____

_____

_____

_____

11 What would you regret doing if Christ returned tonight?

_____

_____

_____

_____

_____

RESOLVE
to take action

12 What practical steps can you take each week or each day to keep you prepared and watchful for Christ's return?

_____

_____

_____

_____

A Why did Jesus tell his disciples about the future?

B Why would anyone falsely claim to be the Messiah (13:5-6, 21-22)? Who are some false messiahs today?

C How can Christians be deceived (13:22)? What does it mean to be "one who endures to the end" (13:13)?

D Why does God allow believers to suffer and be persecuted?

E When have you been tempted to give up following Christ? What keeps you going?

MORE
for studying
other themes
in this section

LESSON 12
WAKING UP TO REALITY
MARK 14:1-72

REFLECT
on your life

1 Describe a time when you were shocked to discover that something had taken place near you without your being aware of it.

_____

_____

_____

_____

_____

READ
the passage

Read Mark 14:1-72 and the following notes:

❐ 14:4, 5   ❐ 14:10   ❐ 14:27-31   ❐ 14:50   ❐ 14:60-64   ❐ 14:71

2 How could the disciples fall asleep that evening knowing that Jesus was so distressed (14:32-42)?

_____

_____

_____

_____

3 How could the disciples desert Jesus after vowing only a few hours earlier to die with him (14:50)?

_____

_____

_____

_____

4 On the eve of this crucial event in human history, we see a whole spectrum of responses from the people involved in this story. Complete the chart with a similar response of Christians today.

At that time	*Today*
Mary worshiped	people worship by
Judas betrayed	people betray by
the disciples slept	people sleep by
Peter disowned	people disown by
Caiaphas plotted	people plot against others by

The disciples slept through Jesus' last few hours, time that could have been spent in preparation. Soon they would face the most difficult days of their lives. How could they have been so oblivious? How could they have neglected to pray at such an important moment? Even more sobering is that under the same conditions, we probably would have fared no better. So the question for us is, how can we wake up? How can we avoid this same spiritual lethargy? The antidote is to get a good dose of reality. Listen carefully to the words of Jesus. Take a hard look at the needs of others around you. Ask God to help you remain faithful in prayer. In other words, take life as seriously as the disciples should have that night. If you don't, you may wake up one day to discover that you slept through the revolution.

R
REALIZE
the principle

5 How do Christians sleep through the revolution today?

_____

_____

_____

6 What does it mean to take life seriously?

_____

_____

_____

_____

7 Why is it difficult to identify with Christ and stand up boldly for him under pressure?

_____

_____

_____

_____

RESPOND
to the message

8 When have you been most alert to the work God is doing in the world around you?

_____

_____

_____

_____

9 What are the cares and concerns of this world that tend to distract you from being more alert spiritually?

_____

_____

_____

_____

10 What are some of the physical distractions that make it difficult for you to pray?

_____

_____

_____

_____

11 What would it take to get you to recognize that time is running out and that you need to wake up to the spiritual realities around you?

RESOLVE
to take action

_____

_____

_____

_____

A The response of Simon's dinner guests when Mary anointed Jesus reflected their values (14:3-9). What were their values? Why were they upset? What "expensive perfume" of yours, if given to God in worship, would draw a similar reaction from others?

MORE
for studying
other themes
in this section

B How did Jesus demonstrate courage during the final days of his life (14:1-72)? In what circumstances can you demonstrate more courage?

C Why do you think each disciple asked Jesus if he was the one who would betray him (14:19)?

D Why did Jesus agonize over his task (14:32-42)?

E Why did the disciples desert Jesus when he was taken (14:50-52)?

F Why did Peter follow far behind? What must he have thought and felt? Why did Peter cry after he denied knowing Christ? In what ways have you disowned Christ?

LESSON 13
UP FROM THE GRAVE HE AROSE
MARK 15:1–16:20

R
REFLECT
on your life

1 The disciples hid, but the women watched from a distance as Joseph and Nicodemus took Jesus' body down from the cross. As you think about the crucifixion scene, how close would you have dared to come?

_____

_____

_____

_____

R
READ
the passage

Read Mark 15:1–16:20 and the following notes:

❏ 15:1 ❏ 15:13 ❏ 15:15 ❏ 15:26 ❏ 15:31 ❏ 15:42ff ❏ 15:44 ❏ 16:6

2 Why was Jesus tried first by the Jews and then by the Romans?

_____

_____

_____

_____

_____

3 What could have motivated the soldiers to treat Jesus so maliciously (15:16-20)?

_____

_____

_____

_____

4 What could have motivated the spectators to ridicule Jesus so relentlessly (15:29-32)?

_____

_____

_____

_____

5 After hearing all of Jesus' predictions, why did the disciples stubbornly refuse to believe the eyewitnesses who saw Jesus alive after he rose from the dead (16:13-14)?

_____

_____

_____

_____

6 Why might it have been a hard decision for Joseph of Arimathea to ask Pilate for permission to take Jesus' body?

_____

_____

_____

_____

Jesus was not simply a talented teacher who ran into some bad luck, or someone with good ideas who got caught in the middle. Jesus was the sinless Son of God who was fulfilling his mission of paying for our sins. Couldn't this terrible experience have been avoided? Couldn't God have simply forgiven humanity? That might have been possible if we had merely hurt God's feelings or violated his personal rights. But we broke his laws, and a penalty had to be paid. If a mass murderer said, "I'm sorry, and I won't do it anymore," we might be able to forgive him, but a legal price would still have to be paid. Jesus paid the price for our sins through his death, and his resurrection shows us clearly that he successfully accomplished what he came to do. Now forgiveness for our sins is possible.

REALIZE
the principle

7 How would Christianity be different if Jesus had remained dead?

_____

_____

_____

_____

8 Why is it easy to forget that all of our sins are forgiven?

RESPOND
to the message

_____

_____

_____

_____

_____

_____

9 How does the Resurrection build your confidence or courage?

_____

_____

_____

_____

_____

10 It's easy to forget that all our sins were nailed to the cross with Christ, even the future ones. God's forgiveness of our sins through Christ is complete. How does this affect the way you live?

_____

_____

_____

_____

_____

_____

11 What can you do to show your gratitude for God's wonderful plan and Christ's profound act of sacrificial love?

RESOLVE
to take action

_____

_____

_____

_____

_____

A Why did Jesus say so little to Pilate (15:2-5)?

B In what way does Barabbas symbolize us today (15:7-15)?

C Why was Jesus sentenced to die on the cross (15:6-15)? How do we know that Jesus truly died and did not just lose consciousness (15:37-39, 44-45)? Why did Jesus die (1 Corinthians 15:3)?

D How did the following people at the cross respond to Jesus (15:25-41): Simon? the two thieves? the soldiers? onlookers? Roman officers? women? With which response do you most identify? Why?

E Why would the women make the trip to the tomb without knowing how they were going to get in (16:2-3)?

F What evidence do we have that Jesus really rose from the dead (16:4-8)? (Also see 15:42-47.)

G Compare the character of the disciples before and after the Resurrection. In what ways did they change? In what ways have you changed because of following Christ?

MORE
for studying
other themes
in this section

Take Your Bible Study to the Next Level

The **Life Application Study Bible** helps you apply truths in God's Word to everyday life. It's packed with nearly 10,000 notes and features that make it today's #1–selling study Bible.

Life Application Notes: Thousands of Life Application notes help explain God's Word and challenge you to apply the truth of Scripture to your life.

Personality Profiles: You can benefit from the life experiences of over a hundred Bible figures.

Book Introductions: These provide vital statistics, an overview, and a timeline to help you quickly understand the message of each book.

Maps: Over 200 maps next to the Bible text highlight important Bible places and events.

Christian Worker's Resource: Enhance your ministry effectiveness with this practical supplement.

Charts: Over 260 charts help explain difficult concepts and relationships.

Harmony of the Gospels: Using a unique numbering system, the events from all four Gospels are harmonized into one chronological account.

Daily Reading Plan: This reading plan is your guide to reading through the entire Bible in one unforgettable year.

Topical Index: A master index provides instant access to Bible passages and features that address the topics on your mind.

Dictionary/Concordance: With entries for many of the important words in the Bible, this is an excellent starting place for studying the Bible text.

Available in the New Living Translation, New International Version, King James Version, and New King James Version. Take an interactive tour of the *Life Application Study Bible* at
www.NewLivingTranslation.com/LASB

CP0271